B_____

TRAVEL GUIDE 2025 AND BEYOND

A Journey Through Culture, Hidden Gems, Cuisine and Local Secrets of this Tropical Paradise on the Eastern Coast of Central America– Packed with Detailed Maps & Itinerary Planner

BY

JAMES W. PATRICK

Copyright © 2024 by James W. Patrick. All rights reserved. The content of this work, including but not limited to text, images, and other media, is owned by James W. Patrick and is protected under copyright laws and international agreements. No part of this work may be reproduced, shared, or transmitted in any form or by any means without the explicit written consent of James W. Patrick. Unauthorized use, duplication, or distribution of this material may lead to legal action, including both civil and criminal penalties. For permission requests or further inquiries, please reach out to the author via the contact details provided in the book or on the author's official page.

TABLE OF CONTENTS

Copyright..1
My Experience in Belize...5
Benefits of this Guide...7

Chapter 1: Introduction to Belize...10
1.1 Welcome to Belize...10
1.2 History and Culture...11
1.3 Geography and Climate...13
1.4 Getting to Belize..14
1.5 Belize for First Time Travelers...16

Chapter 2: Accommodation Options...18
2.1 Luxury Resorts and Hotels..19
2.2 Budget-Friendly Options...20
2.3 Vacation Rentals and Apartments...22
2.4 Camping in Belize...24
2.5 Boutique Hotels...26
2.6 Unique Stays: Eco-Lodges and Island Resorts...............................28

Chapter 3: Transportation...31
3.1 Getting Around Belize...31
3.2 Public Transportation Options..32
3.3 Car Rentals and Driving Tips...33
3.4 Water Taxis and Boat Tours...36
3.5 Domestic Flights and Air Services...38

Chapter 4: Top 10 Attractions & Hidden Gems...................................41
4.1 Belize Barrier Reef...42
4.2 Blue Hole..44
4.3 Ambergris Caye..46

2

4.4 Caye Caulker.. 48
4.5 Actun Tunichil Muknal (ATM) Cave.. 50
4.6 Caracol Mayan Ruins... 52
4.7 Lamanai Mayan Ruins... 55
4.8 Placencia Peninsula... 57
4.9 Hopkins Village... 59
4.10 Garifuna Settlements... 61
4.11 Outdoor Activities and Adventures... 63
4.12 Guided Tours and Recommended Tour Operators........................ 65

Chapter 5 Practical Information and Guidance....................................... 66
5.1 Maps and Navigation... 67
5.2 Five Days Itinerary.. 67
5.3 Essential Packing List... 69
5.4 Setting Your Travel Budget... 70
5.5 Visa Requirements and Entry Procedures....................................... 71
5.6 Safety Tips and Emergency Contacts.. 72
5.7 Currency Exchange and Banking Services...................................... 74
5.8 Language, Communication and Useful Phrases.............................. 75
5.9 Shopping in Belize.. 77
5.10 Health and Wellness Centers... 79
5.11 Useful Websites, Mobile Apps and Online Resources.................. 80
5.12 Internet Access and Connectivity.. 82
5.13 Visitor Centers and Tourist Assistance... 83

Chapter 6: Gastronomic Delights.. 84
6.1 Dining Options and Top Restaurants... 84
6.2 Traditional Belizean Cuisine... 88
6.3 Seafood and Fresh Produce... 89
6.4 Cooking Classes and Culinary Tours.. 91
6.5 Local Markets and Street Food... 93
6.6 Nightlife and Entertainment.. 95

Chapter 7: Day Trips and Excursions...97
7.1 Guatemala Border and Tikal Ruins.. 98
7.2 Mexico Border and Chetumal... 100
7.3 Honduras Bay Islands..102

Chapter 8: Events and Festivals.. 105
8.1 Costa Maya Festival.. 105
8.2 Belize City Carnival Road March.. 107
8.3 Garifuna Settlement Day... 109
8.4 Lobster Fest... 110
8.5 Christmas in Belize..112
Insider Tips and Recommendations... 115

MY EXPERIENCE IN BELIZE

My journey to Belize was nothing short of a transformative experience, a deep dive into a hidden paradise where nature and history converge in ways that few places on earth can replicate. As someone who has spent years traversing the world and immersing myself in various cultures, Belize stands out as a destination that offers a unique blend of natural beauty, ancient wonders, and vibrant local culture. From the moment I stepped foot on its shores, I felt an immediate connection to this small yet incredibly diverse country, and my time there only deepened that bond. One of my first encounters with Belize's magic was on the island of Ambergris Caye, a picturesque Caribbean escape surrounded by the stunning waters of the Belize Barrier Reef. Having been an avid diver for years, I thought I had seen my fair share of underwater ecosystems, but Belize's reef system quickly shattered my expectations. Snorkeling at Hol Chan Marine Reserve was like entering a different realm, where schools of vibrant fish swirled in every direction and the corals seemed to pulse with life. The water was so clear that it felt as though I was floating above an intricate, colorful city. Swimming alongside sea turtles, rays, and even harmless nurse sharks, I was filled with a sense of awe and tranquility. Belize's marine life is a treasure that must be experienced firsthand to truly appreciate its magnificence.

Yet, Belize is not only about its stunning waters. The country's rich history is just as captivating, especially for someone like me who finds solace and fascination in ancient civilizations. A visit to the Maya ruins was at the top of my list, and my time at Xunantunich was a surreal experience. Standing at the base of the El Castillo pyramid, I was immediately enveloped by a sense of awe. The towering structure, built centuries ago, seemed to defy time, as did the surrounding jungle that whispered stories of the past. Climbing to the top, I was rewarded with a breathtaking view of the dense jungle canopy stretching far into Guatemala. The sense of standing in a place where the Maya once thrived was both humbling and exhilarating. It was as if history had come alive, speaking through the stones and trees. Belize also holds a secret within its caves, and my exploration of Actun Tunichil Muknal (ATM) was one of the most adventurous and spiritual experiences I've had. From the moment I swam through the cave's narrow entrance, I was thrust into an underground world that was both haunting and awe-inspiring. As I waded through its chilly waters and carefully navigated its tight passages, I couldn't help but feel a deep respect for the ancient Maya who had used this cave for ritualistic purposes. Inside, I came face-to-face with centuries-old artifacts and the skeletal remains of sacrificial victims, including the famous "Crystal Maiden," whose bones had been calcified over time, giving them a ghostly, glittering appearance. It was a visceral reminder of the deep connection between the Maya and the spiritual world. The experience was more than just a cave exploration — it was a journey through time, a glimpse into the mystical world of the Maya.

However, Belize's beauty extends far beyond its historical sites and marine life. One of my most cherished memories is hiking through the Cockscomb Basin Wildlife Sanctuary, the world's first jaguar preserve. Though I didn't have the fortune of spotting one of these elusive big cats, the jungle itself was a marvel. Every corner of the rainforest was alive with the sounds of howler monkeys, the flutter of colorful birds, and the rustle of leaves underfoot. As I hiked deeper into the sanctuary, I felt an overwhelming sense of peace, as if the jungle had absorbed the frantic pace of modern life and replaced it with the rhythm of nature. The sanctuary's waterfalls and hidden trails felt like treasures waiting to be discovered, and each step further cemented my love for Belize's wild, untamed landscapes. What truly rounded out my experience in Belize was the people. The country's cultural diversity is remarkable, with vibrant communities of Maya, Garifuna, Creole, and Mestizo, each contributing to the rich cultural tapestry of the nation. I vividly remember a warm afternoon spent in a Garifuna village on the southern coast, where I was welcomed with open arms into a family's home. We shared a traditional meal of hudut, a flavorful fish stew served with mashed plantains, while the rhythmic beats of Garifuna drumming echoed in the background. The music, much like the people, was full of life and soul. It was in these moments, sharing meals and stories with locals, that I truly felt the heart of Belize.

Belize may be small, but it is a country that left an indelible mark on my soul. From its awe-inspiring underwater worlds to its ancient ruins and the vibrant cultures that breathe life into every corner, Belize offers an experience that transcends typical travel. It's a place where nature, history, and humanity come together in perfect harmony. I left Belize not just with memories but with a deep sense of connection to a land that is as alive with wonder as it is steeped in ancient history. For those seeking a destination that awakens the senses and stirs the soul, Belize is a journey waiting to be taken.

BENEFITS OF THIS GUIDE

This guide is designed to be your ultimate companion in exploring this Central American gem, whether you are an intrepid adventurer, a cultural enthusiast, or a relaxation seeker. Belize, with its diverse offerings from lush jungles to pristine beaches, promises an experience that caters to every type of traveler. Through this comprehensive guide, we will navigate you through every aspect of your journey, ensuring that you are well-prepared to uncover the wonders of Belize.

Maps and Navigation: Understanding Belize's layout and how to get around is crucial for a seamless travel experience. Our guide provides detailed maps that cover major cities, tourist attractions, and key landmarks. Belize is relatively small, making it easier to navigate between its major points of interest. We'll explore how to use these maps effectively, whether you prefer traditional paper maps or digital navigation tools. You'll also find tips on using local transportation options and suggestions for renting a car or hiring guides to enhance your exploration.

Accommodation Options: Belize offers a wide range of accommodation options to suit every budget and preference. From luxurious beachfront resorts and charming boutique hotels to eco-friendly lodges and budget hostels, there's something for everyone. We delve into the best areas to stay in, including bustling Belize City, serene San Pedro, and the cultural hub of Cayo. Detailed reviews and recommendations will help you choose accommodations that match your travel style and needs, ensuring a comfortable and memorable stay.

Transportation: Getting around Belize is part of the adventure. Our guide covers all transportation options, including domestic flights, bus services, and water taxis. We'll provide insights into the pros and cons of each mode of transport, helping you decide the best way to reach remote locations and popular tourist spots. Whether you're planning a self-drive exploration or relying on public transport, you'll find practical tips and contact information to make your travel efficient and enjoyable.

Top Attractions: Belize is renowned for its breathtaking natural beauty and historical significance. Our guide highlights the top attractions, including the majestic Mayan ruins of Tikal and Caracol, the stunning barrier reef for snorkeling and diving, and the vibrant town of San Ignacio. We'll also cover lesser-known gems that offer unique experiences away from the crowds. Detailed descriptions, visiting tips, and historical context will enrich your understanding and appreciation of these sites.

Practical Information and Travel Resources: Navigating a new country requires knowing some practical details. Our guide provides essential information such as visa requirements, currency exchange, and health and safety tips. We'll also include emergency contact numbers, local customs, and cultural etiquette to ensure you're well-prepared. Travel resources such as tourist information centers, local guides, and online tools will be featured to assist you throughout your journey.

Culinary Delights: Belizean cuisine is a delightful fusion of flavors influenced by its diverse cultures. From savory seafood dishes and traditional Mayan fare to Caribbean-inspired meals, the culinary landscape is as rich as the country's history. Our guide explores must-try dishes, top restaurants, and local food markets. Discover where to enjoy a fresh ceviche, savor jerk chicken, or indulge in sweet plantains, and get tips on local dining customs and etiquette.

Culture and Heritage: Immerse yourself in Belize's vibrant cultural tapestry. Our guide delves into the country's rich heritage, including its indigenous Maya roots, Afro-Caribbean influences, and colonial past. Learn about traditional festivals, music, dance, and art that shape Belizean identity. We'll highlight cultural events and museums where you can experience and understand the diverse cultural expressions that define Belize.

Outdoor Activities and Adventures: For adventure enthusiasts, Belize offers a plethora of outdoor activities. Our guide covers exhilarating experiences such as exploring the dense rainforests, kayaking through scenic rivers, and hiking to spectacular waterfalls. We'll also provide information on zip-lining, cave tubing, and wildlife spotting. Whether you're seeking high-energy thrills or tranquil nature experiences, Belize has it all.

Shopping: Belizean markets and shops offer unique souvenirs and local crafts. Our guide will help you navigate through the best places to shop for handmade goods, traditional textiles, and local art. Discover where to find authentic Belizean products, such as handmade jewelry, carved wooden items, and traditional garments, ensuring you take home memorable keepsakes from your trip.

Day Trips and Excursions: Exploring Belize extends beyond its major attractions. We'll suggest a range of day trips and excursions that allow you to experience the country's diverse landscapes and hidden treasures. Whether it's a visit to the serene island of Caye Caulker, a trip to the beautiful Blue Hole, or a guided tour of a local nature reserve, our guide will help you plan these excursions efficiently.

Entertainment and Nightlife: When the sun sets, Belize comes alive with a variety of entertainment options. From lively beach bars and vibrant nightclubs to cultural performances and local music venues, our guide covers the best spots for evening fun. Discover where to enjoy a night of dancing, live music, or a relaxing drink by the sea, and get insights into the local nightlife scene.

CHAPTER 1
INTRODUCTION TO BELIZE

1.1 Welcome to Belize

Welcome to Belize, a tropical paradise located on the eastern coast of Central America, bordered by Mexico to the north, Guatemala to the west and south, and the stunning Caribbean Sea to the east. Known for its pristine beaches, lush jungles, and ancient Mayan ruins, Belize offers a diverse experience that seamlessly blends adventure, history, and relaxation. As the only Central American country where English is the official language, communication is easy for international travelers, making Belize an accessible and welcoming destination. For first-time visitors, Belize City is often the primary entry point, as it houses the country's largest airport. While Belize City itself serves more as a transit hub, it offers glimpses into the country's colonial past with its historic architecture and vibrant markets. However, most travelers are drawn to Belize's surrounding areas, such as the world-famous Belize Barrier Reef, a UNESCO World Heritage Site. Just offshore, the reef beckons divers and snorkelers from around the globe, eager to explore its underwater marvels, teeming with marine life and colorful coral formations.

Visitors should be aware that Belize operates on a relatively laid-back schedule, with public transportation options like buses, taxis, and water taxis being available but often running without strict time tables. For those looking to venture inland, the country's expansive rainforests offer incredible opportunities for wildlife viewing, hiking, and exploring hidden waterfalls. Adventurous spirits can also discover caves once used by the ancient Maya for ceremonial purposes, such as the famous Actun Tunichil Muknal Cave, where visitors can still see ancient artifacts and skeletal remains. The local currency, the Belizean dollar, is easily exchanged with US dollars, which are widely accepted. The food scene in Belize reflects its rich cultural diversity, with influences from Caribbean, Creole, and Mayan cuisine, ensuring a culinary adventure for every visitor. Safety in Belize is generally good, but travelers should exercise caution, particularly in Belize City, where some areas are known for petty crime. As with any travel, common-sense precautions are advised. Ultimately, Belize offers a perfect mix of relaxation and adventure, where visitors can spend their mornings exploring ancient ruins or jungles and their afternoons lounging on a tropical beach. With its natural beauty, warm hospitality, and rich cultural tapestry, Belize promises a journey filled with unforgettable experiences for any traveler.

1.2 History and Culture

The Ancient Roots of Belize
The history of Belize stretches back thousands of years, with the ancient Maya civilization being one of its earliest inhabitants. The Maya left behind a wealth of archaeological treasures, from towering pyramids to intricately carved stelae, which today remain as silent witnesses to a once-thriving empire. These ruins, like Caracol and Xunantunich, offer visitors a chance to explore sacred sites deep within the jungle, where ancient temples still rise above the canopy. The Maya were not just builders but also skilled astronomers, mathematicians, and artists, whose influence continues to shape Belize's cultural landscape. Their legacy endures not only in the ruins but also in the cultural practices and traditions of modern-day Belizean communities.

Colonial Influences and the Birth of a Nation
Belize's colonial history began with European explorers, particularly the Spanish and British, who vied for control over its resources. British settlers established the country as a haven for logwood, a valuable timber resource, eventually leading to its designation as British Honduras. This colonial past is visible in the architecture of Belize City, with its old wooden buildings and

government structures reflecting a British influence. Despite Spanish claims to the territory, it was the British who maintained a stronghold, and Belize eventually gained independence from Britain in 1981. This period of colonial rule has left an indelible mark on Belize's culture, particularly in its language, legal system, and education.

A Cultural Tapestry of Diversity
Belize is a melting pot of cultures, where diverse communities live together harmoniously, creating a vibrant cultural tapestry. From the descendants of the Maya and Garifuna to Creole, Mestizo, and Mennonite communities, the country is a living example of cultural coexistence. Each group brings its own unique traditions, music, and cuisine, contributing to the rich cultural experience visitors can enjoy. The Garifuna people, with their Afro-Caribbean roots, are known for their drumming, dance, and storytelling traditions, which visitors can witness in southern Belizean towns like Dangriga. Similarly, the influence of Creole culture is evident in the spoken language and local cuisine, where dishes like rice and beans are staples of daily life.

Belizean Festivals and Traditions
Festivals in Belize are a colorful and lively celebration of the country's diverse heritage. From the Garifuna Settlement Day to the Belize Carnival, these events bring together communities in a shared display of joy and pride. During these festivals, visitors can experience traditional dances, music, and even join in the celebrations, making it a perfect way to engage with the local culture. The annual Belize International Film Festival showcases the country's growing arts scene, while the Maya Deer Dance and other indigenous rituals provide insight into ancient spiritual practices. These festivals offer a glimpse into the soul of Belize, where history and culture are intertwined in the daily lives of its people.

The Spirit of Belize Today
Modern Belize is a unique blend of ancient heritage and contemporary culture, where the past coexists harmoniously with the present. While the country continues to evolve, its deep respect for nature and tradition remains at the heart of Belizean life. English is widely spoken, making it easy for travelers to connect with locals and learn about their stories, while the laid-back pace of life encourages visitors to slow down and truly immerse themselves in their surroundings. Whether exploring its rich history or experiencing its vibrant culture firsthand, Belize offers an authentic experience that is both enriching and

unforgettable. Travelers are welcomed with open arms, invited to discover a country where the echoes of the past resonate in the rhythms of the present.

1.3 Geography and Climate

Geography of Belize

Belize, located on the northeastern coast of Central America, boasts a diverse landscape that captivates visitors with its striking beauty. The Caribbean Sea gently kisses its eastern shores, where white-sand beaches stretch as far as the eye can see. Inland, the geography transforms into lush tropical rainforests, filled with towering trees, rushing rivers, and hidden caves. The Maya Mountains dominate the southern region, adding dramatic peaks and rolling valleys to the terrain. Belize's western border touches Guatemala, where dense jungles hold ancient ruins and a rich ecosystem waiting to be explored.

Coastal Wonders and Islands

Belize is renowned for its magnificent coastlines and the world's second-largest barrier reef, which lies just offshore. The crystal-clear waters of the Caribbean invite snorkelers and divers to immerse themselves in the vibrant marine life. Scattered across the waters are numerous cayes—small islands—each with its unique charm, offering tranquil getaways. Ambergris Caye and Caye Caulker are two of the most popular, featuring palm-fringed beaches and colorful coral gardens. The turquoise waters around these islands teem with tropical fish, making Belize a paradise for water sports enthusiasts.

Rainforests and Wildlife

The inland geography of Belize is dominated by tropical rainforests that provide a haven for an incredible variety of wildlife. Jaguars, howler monkeys, and toucans are just a few of the creatures that roam the forests, making the country a dream destination for nature lovers. These rainforests also shelter a wealth of medicinal plants and exotic orchids, painting the landscape with rich hues of green and splashes of vibrant color. Trekking through the jungle trails leads visitors to hidden waterfalls, ancient Mayan sites, and an overwhelming sense of being surrounded by pure, untouched nature.

The Maya Mountains and Caves

The rugged Maya Mountains in southern Belize add a distinct flavor to the country's geography, their peaks often shrouded in mist. These mountains are home to dense forests, rich in biodiversity and natural beauty. Below the surface, the limestone landscape gives way to vast cave systems that have historical and cultural significance. Visitors can explore these mystical caves, many of which were used by the ancient Maya for religious ceremonies. The Actun Tunichil Muknal cave is particularly famous for its archaeological treasures, including skeletons, ceramics, and stone artifacts.

Climate of Belize

Belize enjoys a tropical climate that varies slightly depending on the region, with warm temperatures throughout the year. Coastal areas remain consistently balmy, tempered by the cool Caribbean breezes, making it ideal for beach lovers. The dry season, from November to April, is the most popular time for visitors, offering sunny days and clear skies. From June to November, the rainy season brings lush greenery, though storms and hurricanes are occasional risks. Whether basking in the sun or marveling at the power of tropical rains, visitors will find Belize's climate to be an integral part of its allure.

1.4 Getting to Belize

Belize, a tropical paradise located on the Caribbean coast of Central America, is a dream destination for travelers seeking adventure, culture, and stunning natural beauty. Known for its vibrant marine life, ancient Mayan ruins, and lush jungles, getting to Belize is an exciting journey in itself.

Getting to Belize by Air Travel

Air travel is undoubtedly the most convenient and popular way to reach Belize, particularly for international visitors. The Philip S.W. Goldson International Airport, located just outside Belize City, serves as the primary gateway, welcoming flights from major cities across North America and beyond. Airlines such as American Airlines, Delta, United, and Southwest offer regular direct flights, with ticket prices varying based on the season and how far in advance you book. Generally, travelers can expect round-trip fares to range from $300 to $700, depending on their departure city and the time of year. Booking can easily be done through airline websites or popular travel platforms, allowing for seamless planning.

Traveling by Train to Belize

While Belize does not have an extensive train network, adventurous travelers might find options to reach the country by rail from neighboring Guatemala. The scenic train journey through Guatemala offers a glimpse of lush landscapes and vibrant cultures before crossing the border into Belize. Visitors can take a train from cities like Antigua or Guatemala City to reach the border town of Melchor de Mencos. After crossing the border, a short taxi or bus ride will connect you to various destinations in Belize. Though not as direct as flying, this route provides a unique opportunity to experience the beauty of Central America.

Road Travel to Belize
For those already traveling within Central America, entering Belize by road can be an exhilarating experience. Several border crossings allow access from Mexico and Guatemala, with the most frequented being the Chetumal border from Mexico and the Melchor de Mencos border from Guatemala. Buses run regularly from major cities like Cancún or Guatemala City, offering budget-friendly options for travelers. The journey through picturesque landscapes enhances the travel experience, with opportunities to stop at small towns and local eateries along the way. Once in Belize, well-maintained roads provide access to various regions, making road travel a great way to explore.

Booking Travel and Prices
Booking tickets, whether for flights or buses, is easy thanks to online booking platforms and official websites of airlines and bus companies. Air tickets can be secured through platforms such as Expedia (https://www.expedia.com/) or directly through airline websites like American Airlines (https://www.aa.com/) or United (https://www.united.com/). For bus travel, companies like ADO in Mexico offer services to Belize, and tickets can be booked online or at bus stations. Prices fluctuate based on season and availability, so it's recommended to book well in advance, especially during peak travel periods. Comparing fares across multiple platforms helps secure the best deals.

Crossing the Borders
When traveling by land, visitors should be aware of the necessary documentation required for crossing borders. A valid passport is essential, and travelers may need to show proof of onward travel or sufficient funds. Border fees can vary, so it's wise to have some cash on hand for these charges. The customs process can be straightforward, but patience is key as queues may form. Ensuring that all travel documents are organized will make crossing into Belize smoother, allowing you to fully enjoy the adventure that awaits.

Important Information for Visitors

Visitors should consider the best time of year to travel, as peak seasons can drive up prices. Belize is a popular destination, especially during the winter months when tourists flock to enjoy its tropical climate. It's essential to have all necessary documents, including passports and any required visas, ready before embarking on the journey. Whether by air, road, or a combination of transportation modes, the journey to Belize can be as exciting as the destination itself, offering multiple options for every type of traveler.

1.5 Belize for First Time Travelers

Belize, a small but vibrant country on the northeastern coast of Central America, offers first-time travelers an enchanting mix of natural beauty, rich history, and warm hospitality. Known for its tropical climate and diverse geography, Belize captivates visitors with its pristine beaches, dense rainforests, and ancient Mayan ruins. The country's official language is English, making communication easy for many international travelers. Whether you're drawn by the allure of the Caribbean Sea or the mysteries of the jungle, Belize offers a wealth of experiences for every type of traveler.

Belize City

Belize City, the country's former capital and largest urban center, serves as the primary point of entry for most visitors. While it may not have the glitzy appeal of other tourist destinations, Belize City is a cultural hub filled with historical landmarks and lively markets. For first-time visitors, it's important to note that the city can be bustling and chaotic, especially during peak travel seasons. However, its central location makes it a convenient starting point for exploring the country's most famous attractions, including the nearby cayes, the Belize Barrier Reef, and inland excursions to the Maya Mountains.

Cultural Insights for Travelers

Travelers will quickly notice that Belize is a melting pot of cultures, with a diverse population that includes Creole, Maya, Garifuna, Mestizo, and other ethnic groups. Each community adds its unique flavor to the country's rich cultural tapestry, influencing everything from language to cuisine. Visitors should be prepared for a relaxed pace of life, where things often run on "Belize time"—a laid-back attitude that can sometimes mean delays but always reflects the country's easygoing charm. Tasting the local cuisine is a must, with dishes like rice and beans, stewed chicken, and fresh seafood offering a delicious introduction to Belizean culture.

Safety and Practical Tips
Belize is generally safe for travelers, but like any destination, it's important to exercise caution, especially in Belize City. Travelers should stick to well-populated areas, avoid walking alone at night, and secure their belongings. Hiring a licensed guide for excursions is recommended, as they offer not only protection but also valuable insights into Belize's natural wonders and cultural history. When traveling to the islands or more remote areas, it's always good to inform someone of your plans. Most locals are friendly and welcoming, but having a basic awareness of your surroundings will ensure a smooth and enjoyable trip.

Getting Around Belize
Transportation in Belize is varied, with options ranging from domestic flights and water taxis to buses and rental cars. Belize City serves as the main transportation hub, with frequent ferries departing to popular islands like Ambergris Caye and Caye Caulker. For inland travel, buses and private shuttles are the most common means of getting around, though adventurous travelers might opt to rent a car to explore at their own pace. Roads can be bumpy in more rural areas, so it's advisable to rent a four-wheel-drive vehicle if you plan on venturing off the beaten path. Whether by land or sea, traveling in Belize is an adventure in itself, offering breathtaking views along the way.

Final Thoughts for First-Time Visitors
For those visiting Belize for the first time, the country is a perfect blend of adventure and relaxation. From the stunning coral reefs to the mysteries of ancient ruins, Belize offers countless opportunities for exploration. Its laid-back atmosphere and friendly locals make it an inviting destination, whether you're snorkeling off the coast or hiking through the jungle. By embracing the rhythm of life in Belize, travelers will discover a hidden gem in Central America that offers unforgettable experiences at every turn.

CHAPTER 2
ACCOMMODATION OPTIONS

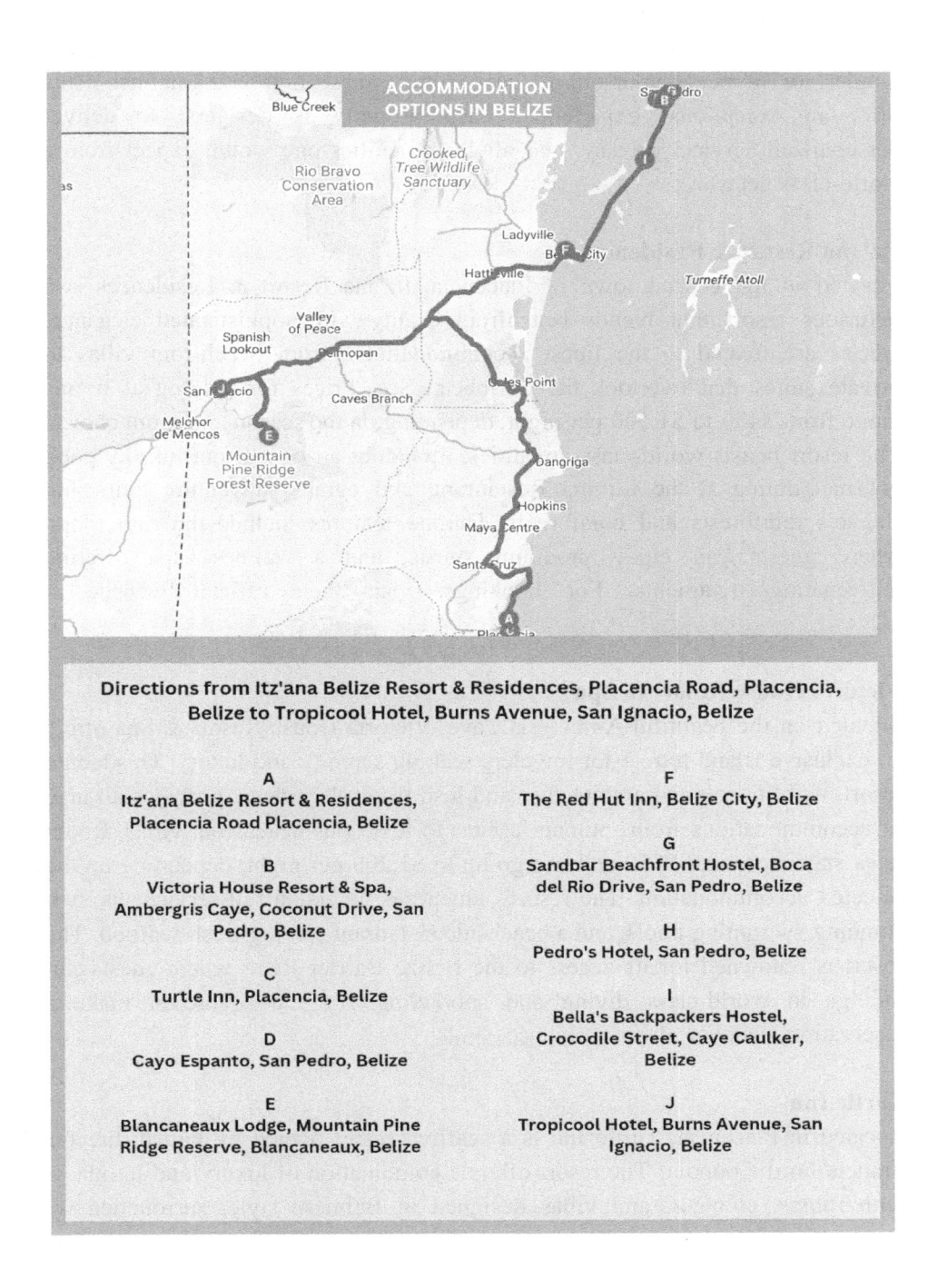

ACCOMMODATION OPTIONS IN BELIZE

Directions from Itz'ana Belize Resort & Residences, Placencia Road, Placencia, Belize to Tropicool Hotel, Burns Avenue, San Ignacio, Belize

A
Itz'ana Belize Resort & Residences, Placencia Road Placencia, Belize

B
Victoria House Resort & Spa, Ambergris Caye, Coconut Drive, San Pedro, Belize

C
Turtle Inn, Placencia, Belize

D
Cayo Espanto, San Pedro, Belize

E
Blancaneaux Lodge, Mountain Pine Ridge Reserve, Blancaneaux, Belize

F
The Red Hut Inn, Belize City, Belize

G
Sandbar Beachfront Hostel, Boca del Rio Drive, San Pedro, Belize

H
Pedro's Hotel, San Pedro, Belize

I
Bella's Backpackers Hostel, Crocodile Street, Caye Caulker, Belize

J
Tropicool Hotel, Burns Avenue, San Ignacio, Belize

2.1 Luxury Resorts and Hotels

For travelers seeking more than just adventure, Belize's luxury hotels and resorts provide an opulent escape, blending modern comfort with the raw beauty of the country's landscapes. Whether you're looking to relax by the sea, explore exotic jungles, or immerse yourself in local culture, these high-end establishments offer an exceptional experience. Each property is designed to deliver personalized service, privacy, and all the amenities one would expect from a world-class getaway.

Itz'ana Resort & Residences

Located in the coastal town of Placencia, Itz'ana Resort & Residences is a luxurious resort that blends beachfront beauty with sophisticated elegance. Guests are treated to the finest accommodations, from beachfront villas to private suites that overlook the Caribbean Sea. Prices for lodging at Itz'ana range from $400 to $1,500 per night, depending on the season and room choice. The resort boasts world-class amenities, including an oceanfront infinity pool, gourmet dining at the Limilia Restaurant, and curated adventure tours into Belize's rainforests and coral reefs. Unique features include the rum room, where guests can enjoy premium spirits, and a wellness spa offering rejuvenating treatments. For bookings, visit their official website at www.itzanabelize.com.

Victoria House Resort & Spa

Situated on the beautiful Ambergris Caye, Victoria House Resort & Spa offers an exclusive island retreat for travelers seeking serenity and luxury. This iconic resort, with its colonial architecture and lush tropical gardens, provides a range of accommodations from intimate casitas to luxurious beachfront villas. Room rates start at around $350 and can go up to $1,200 per night, depending on the selected accommodation. The resort's amenities include a full-service spa, two stunning swimming pools, and a beachside restaurant serving fresh seafood. The resort is renowned for its access to the Belize Barrier Reef, where guests can indulge in world-class diving and snorkeling. To learn more or make a reservation, visit www.victoria-house.com.

Turtle Inn

Located in Placencia, Turtle Inn is a seafront resort owned by famed director Francis Ford Coppola. The resort offers a combination of luxury and intimacy, with rooms, cottages, and villas designed in Balinese style, surrounded by tropical gardens. Rates at Turtle Inn vary from $500 to $1,500 per night. Guests can enjoy exquisite dining experiences at the Mare Restaurant, known for its fresh seafood and Italian-inspired dishes, as well as a range of activities, including scuba diving, snorkeling, and sailing. Turtle Inn also features an organic garden and a wellness spa offering traditional Thai massages. For bookings and more details, visit their official website at www.thefamilycoppolahideaways.com.

Cayo Espanto
For travelers seeking the ultimate private island experience, Cayo Espanto is a five-star luxury resort located off the coast of Ambergris Caye. This exclusive resort features seven villas, each with its private pool and dedicated staff. The price for staying at Cayo Espanto ranges from $1,695 to over $3,000 per night, offering unparalleled privacy and luxury. Guests enjoy personalized service, gourmet dining tailored to their preferences, and access to water sports such as sailing, snorkeling, and kayaking. The island is ideal for those looking to escape the crowds and immerse themselves in tranquility. Reservations can be made through their website at www.aprivateisland.com.

Blancaneaux Lodge
Blancaneaux Lodge, another Coppola-owned retreat, is located in the Mountain Pine Ridge Forest Reserve, offering a luxurious rainforest escape. Surrounded by waterfalls and natural pools, this eco-lodge offers a unique blend of luxury and sustainability. Accommodations include riverside cabanas and luxury villas, with prices starting from $450 to $1,200 per night. The lodge features organic gardens, a farm-to-table restaurant, and a spa that offers treatments using locally sourced ingredients. Its proximity to ancient Maya ruins and nature trails makes it perfect for adventure seekers looking to combine comfort with exploration. For more information, visit their official site at www.thefamilycoppolahideaways.com.

2.2 Budget-Friendly Options

Belize, while known for its luxury resorts and eco-lodges, also offers a wide range of affordable accommodations for budget-conscious travelers. From cozy hostels to charming hotels, there are plenty of places that provide excellent service, comfortable lodging, and the opportunity to experience the country's rich culture without breaking the bank.

The Red Hut Inn
Located just outside of Belize City, The Red Hut Inn is a budget-friendly hotel that offers a peaceful atmosphere and easy access to the city's attractions. With rates starting around $50 per night, it's ideal for those who want to stay close to the city without the hustle and bustle. The rooms are simple yet clean and comfortable, with air conditioning, Wi-Fi, and cable TV. The inn also has a shared kitchen where guests can prepare their meals, adding to its affordability. The owners are known for their warm hospitality and often arrange tours for guests. For bookings and more information, visit http://red-hut-inn-belize.50megs.com/.

Sandbar Beachfront Hostel and Restaurant
Located on the popular island of Ambergris Caye, Sandbar Beachfront Hostel and Restaurant offers budget travelers a beachfront experience without the hefty price tag. Dorm beds start at around $15 per night, while private rooms begin at $70, making it a great option for both backpackers and budget-conscious couples. The hostel features a lively on-site restaurant and bar, a perfect spot for socializing and meeting fellow travelers. Guests can enjoy amenities like free Wi-Fi, a pool, and discounted water sports. Its location also provides easy access to snorkeling and diving trips along the Belize Barrier Reef. To make reservations, visit www.sandbarhostel.com.

Yuma's House Belize
Yuma's House Belize is a popular backpacker hostel located in Caye Caulker, known for its laid-back island vibe and affordable accommodations. Rooms at Yuma's House start at $20 for dormitory-style lodging, and the hostel's proximity to the beach makes it a great place for travelers who want to relax by the sea. The hostel has a large communal area, hammocks for lounging, and a shared kitchen, providing an ideal space for socializing with fellow travelers. Its convenient location allows guests to easily explore Caye Caulker's stunning beaches, take boat tours, or enjoy the local nightlife. For booking information, visit https://yumas-house-belize.hotels-belize.com/.

Pedro's Hotel
Pedro's Hotel in San Pedro, Ambergris Caye, is another excellent option for budget travelers. With rates starting at just $45 per night, Pedro's offers simple but comfortable rooms equipped with Wi-Fi and air conditioning. The hotel is known for its lively, fun atmosphere, with an on-site bar and pizzeria that often

hosts social events. Pedro's also has two pools and is located just a short walk from the beach, making it a fantastic option for travelers who want affordable accommodations near the ocean. It's a popular choice for backpackers and young travelers looking for budget-friendly fun. For more details, visit https://pedros.hotels-belize.com/.

Bella's Backpackers
Situated on the tranquil island of Caye Caulker, Bella's Backpackers provides a laid-back, budget-friendly option for those exploring Belize's coastline. The hostel offers both dormitory-style accommodations and private rooms, with prices starting at around $12 per night for dorms. Bella's has a rustic charm, with hammocks scattered throughout and an open communal kitchen. Guests can take part in daily activities organized by the hostel, such as snorkeling tours, sunset cruises, and beach barbecues, making it an excellent base for social and adventurous travelers. For booking and availability, visit https://www.bellasinbelize.com/.

Tropicool Hotel
Located in the heart of San Ignacio, Tropicool Hotel offers clean, comfortable, and budget-friendly accommodations starting at around $30 per night. It's an excellent option for those looking to explore Belize's inland attractions, such as the Maya ruins of Xunantunich and the Mountain Pine Ridge Forest Reserve. The hotel is known for its friendly staff and peaceful courtyard, offering a serene retreat after a day of exploring. With easy access to restaurants, shops, and tour operators, Tropicool is perfect for those wanting to explore San Ignacio without spending too much on accommodations. For bookings, visit https://tropicool.hotels-belize.com/.

2.3 Vacation Rentals and Apartments

For travelers seeking a more intimate and personalized stay, vacation rentals and apartments in Belize provide an ideal option. These accommodations offer a home-like atmosphere with the added benefits of privacy, flexibility, and unique local experiences. Vacation rentals in Belize range from beachfront villas to cozy city apartments, giving visitors a chance to immerse themselves in the country's natural beauty and cultural richness while enjoying all the comforts of home. Whether you're planning a romantic getaway, a family vacation, or a solo adventure, Belize's vacation rentals cater to all tastes and budgets, ensuring a memorable stay.

The Great House Inn Vacation Rental
The Great House Inn, situated in the Fort George area of Belize City, offers a perfect mix of comfort and history. Originally a colonial mansion, this vacation rental provides spacious and elegantly furnished apartments with modern amenities. Guests can enjoy air-conditioned rooms, free Wi-Fi, and access to the lush tropical garden. With prices starting at around $120 per night, the inn is a fantastic choice for those wanting a quiet retreat close to the city's main attractions. The Great House Inn is also a short walk from the waterfront, where travelers can experience Belize's vibrant cultural scene. For more information, visit www.greathousebelize.com.

Royal Palm Island Vacation Rental
Situated on its own private island, Royal Palm Island Resort offers exclusive vacation rentals for those seeking luxury and seclusion. Just a short boat ride from Belize City, this resort features beachfront cottages with stunning views of the Caribbean Sea. With prices starting at $300 per night, each cottage includes spacious living areas, private verandas, and fully equipped kitchens. Guests can enjoy activities such as kayaking, paddleboarding, and snorkeling, as well as pampering themselves with spa treatments. The resort's peaceful ambiance and the beauty of the surrounding nature make it an ideal getaway for couples and families alike. Bookings can be made through https://royal-palm-island-resort.hotels-belize.com/.

El Rey Hotel Vacation Apartments
Located in the heart of Belmopan, El Rey Hotel offers budget-friendly vacation apartments that are perfect for exploring Belize's inland treasures. These apartments start at approximately $80 per night and include amenities like air conditioning, Wi-Fi, and a small kitchenette. The hotel's central location makes it easy to access nearby attractions, such as the Belize Zoo and the Maya ruins of Xunantunich. Guests also appreciate the hotel's friendly and welcoming staff, who are always eager to offer advice on tours and activities. The quiet, relaxed atmosphere makes El Rey Hotel a great choice for those seeking affordable comfort.

Villa Boscardi Vacation Apartment
Located in a quiet residential area of Belize City, Villa Boscardi offers charming vacation apartments perfect for long or short stays. With prices starting at $95 per night, these apartments provide the perfect balance of comfort and

convenience. Each unit is equipped with air conditioning, a kitchenette, and a private bathroom, making it a great option for families or groups. The villa is surrounded by lush gardens and provides easy access to both the city's attractions and the beach. Villa Boscardi's personalized service, peaceful setting, and homely feel make it a popular choice for travelers looking for a relaxing retreat. For more information, visit www.villaboscardi.com.

The Palms Oceanfront Vacation Apartments
The Palms Oceanfront Suites, located on Ambergris Caye, offers luxurious vacation apartments just steps from the beach. These spacious apartments, starting at around $250 per night, feature full kitchens, private balconies, and breathtaking ocean views. Guests can enjoy the hotel's outdoor pool, direct beach access, and complimentary bicycles for exploring the island. The Palms is known for its warm hospitality and attention to detail, ensuring guests have a memorable and relaxing stay. Whether you're here to explore the Belize Barrier Reef or simply unwind by the sea, these vacation apartments provide a perfect blend of luxury and convenience. Bookings can be made through www.belizepalms.com.

Villa Verano Vacation Rental
Villa Verano, located in Hopkins Village, offers upscale vacation rentals ideal for families or groups of friends. These beachfront villas start at $500 per night and feature multiple bedrooms, full kitchens, and private pools. The villa is elegantly designed with a mix of modern and traditional Belizean architecture, providing a luxurious and authentic stay. Guests can enjoy amenities such as a rooftop lounge, spa services, and easy access to activities like snorkeling, fishing, and exploring the nearby jungle. The serene environment and stunning views of the Caribbean Sea make Villa Verano an unforgettable destination.

2.4 Camping in Belize

Camping in Belize offers a unique opportunity for travelers to connect with nature in one of Central America's most biodiverse regions. Whether you're setting up a tent in the lush rainforest, near Mayan ruins, or along the beautiful coastline, Belize offers a range of camping experiences that cater to both the adventurous spirit and the serene nature lover. These sites allow visitors to enjoy the country's natural beauty up close while being enveloped in the peaceful sounds of nature. From backpackers to families seeking a quiet escape, Belize's camping sites provide affordable yet immersive experiences.

Cockscomb Basin Wildlife Sanctuary

Cockscomb Basin Wildlife Sanctuary, located in the Stann Creek District, is renowned for being the world's first jaguar reserve. This expansive sanctuary offers an ideal camping experience for nature lovers who want to explore the rainforest. With camping fees starting at around $10 per night, it's a budget-friendly option for those who don't mind basic amenities like shared restrooms and outdoor showers. What makes camping here particularly exciting is the opportunity to embark on jungle hikes and spot wildlife, including birds, monkeys, and, if you're lucky, even a jaguar. The campgrounds are surrounded by nature trails, waterfalls, and the winding Sittee River, making it a perfect place for explorers.

Mountain Pine Ridge Forest Reserve

Mountain Pine Ridge Forest Reserve, located in the Cayo District, is a haven for those who appreciate cooler temperatures and rugged landscapes. This reserve offers a number of camping spots located among pine trees and near stunning natural attractions such as the Rio On Pools and the Thousand Foot Falls. Prices for camping in the reserve typically range from $5 to $10 per night, making it a very affordable option for those on a budget. Although the reserve is more remote, campers will find basic amenities such as picnic tables and fire pits. The reserve is also home to abundant wildlife and offers opportunities for hiking, bird watching, and even exploring hidden caves. The peaceful environment, combined with the breathtaking views, makes this a popular choice for campers.

Hopkins Bay Resort Beach Camping

For those who wish to camp near the ocean, Hopkins Bay Resort offers beach camping in the laid-back village of Hopkins, located along Belize's Caribbean coast. While the resort provides luxury accommodations, it also offers an affordable beach camping experience starting at around $20 per night. Campers can set up their tents on the sandy shores, with the soothing sounds of the ocean providing a perfect backdrop for a restful night. Facilities include access to shared showers, restrooms, and beachside barbecue pits. What sets this spot apart is the option to enjoy the resort's amenities, such as the beachfront restaurant, while still enjoying the simplicity of camping.

St. Herman's Blue Hole National Park

Located in the Cayo District, St. Herman's Blue Hole National Park is famous for its natural limestone sinkhole and caves. The park offers a unique camping experience where visitors can sleep in the shadows of the Maya Mountains and explore some of Belize's most interesting geological formations. With camping fees around $10 per night, it's an affordable destination for those who enjoy a mix of adventure and tranquility. Campers can explore the park's extensive cave system, swim in the Blue Hole, or hike through the lush rainforest that surrounds the area. The park's campgrounds provide basic facilities, but the natural beauty and nearby attractions more than make up for the lack of luxury amenities.

Bacab Eco Park Camping Grounds
Bacab Eco Park, located just outside Belize City, offers a convenient camping site for those looking for easy access to both nature and urban amenities. This eco-friendly park offers camping grounds with basic facilities, including showers and picnic areas, starting at approximately $15 per night. One of the highlights of camping at Bacab is the access to the park's sprawling natural attractions, such as nature trails and a large swimming pool. The park also provides canoeing and horseback riding activities, making it a great option for families or travelers who want to engage in outdoor recreation. Its proximity to Belize City also makes it ideal for travelers seeking a nature escape without being too far from the city.

Placencia Peninsula Camping Grounds
Located on the picturesque Placencia Peninsula, this camping site offers visitors the chance to experience Belize's coastal beauty while staying on a budget. With prices for beachside camping starting at $15 per night, the camping grounds are an affordable option for those who want to enjoy Placencia's crystal-clear waters and stunning sunsets. The camping grounds provide basic amenities, such as showers, restrooms, and fire pits for cooking, and are located just a short walk from the vibrant village of Placencia. Campers can enjoy snorkeling, swimming, and fishing right from the beach, or take a stroll into town to enjoy the local restaurants and bars. The laid-back atmosphere and stunning views make this one of the best spots for beach camping in Belize.

2.5 Boutique Hotels

Amid the stunning landscapes, Belize is also home to a selection of boutique hotels that provide a personalized and intimate experience. These smaller, independently-owned accommodations stand out for their charm, attention to detail, and unique offerings. For travelers seeking something beyond the typical resort experience, boutique hotels in Belize promise a memorable stay, where comfort meets character, and hospitality is elevated to an art form.

Ka'ana Resort

Located in the lush Cayo District, Ka'ana Resort is a boutique hotel that seamlessly blends luxury with local culture. With rooms starting at around $300 per night, this property offers a range of accommodations from charming casitas to private villas with plunge pools. Ka'ana is renowned for its commitment to sustainability and personalized guest experiences, offering farm-to-table dining and exclusive tours of nearby Maya ruins. The intimate size of the resort ensures that each guest is treated to an unparalleled level of service, whether enjoying the on-site spa, exploring the organic garden, or embarking on guided jungle adventures. For bookings, visit https://www.kaanabelize.com/.

Turtle Inn

Turtle Inn, located in Placencia, offers an enchanting beachfront escape with a unique blend of rustic charm and Balinese influences. Owned by filmmaker Francis Ford Coppola, this boutique hotel features thatched cottages, starting at approximately $350 per night. Each cottage is thoughtfully designed to embrace the natural surroundings, featuring handcrafted furnishings and open-air bathrooms. Turtle Inn provides an array of amenities, including two outdoor pools, a dive shop, and a luxurious spa. Guests can also indulge in world-class dining, with seafood fresh from the Caribbean, all while soaking in the serene beauty of the Placencia Peninsula. For bookings, visit https://thefamilycoppolahideaways.com/resort/turtle-inn/

Victoria House Resort & Spa

On the island of Ambergris Caye, Victoria House Resort & Spa stands as one of Belize's most iconic boutique hotels. Prices for rooms begin at $275 per night, offering accommodations ranging from charming casitas to expansive beachfront villas. Victoria House is known for its timeless elegance, with colonial-style architecture, manicured gardens, and unobstructed views of the Caribbean Sea. Guests can take advantage of amenities such as the resort's full-service spa, beachfront dining, and easy access to the Belize Barrier Reef. The peaceful and secluded atmosphere of Victoria House makes it a favorite among honeymooners and couples looking for a romantic getaway. For bookings, visit

The Lodge at Chaa Creek

The Lodge at Chaa Creek, situated along the Macal River in western Belize, is a premier eco-luxury boutique hotel that offers an interesting jungle experience. Lodging starts at around $250 per night, with options ranging from traditional cottages to luxury treetop villas. Chaa Creek is renowned for its commitment to sustainable tourism, with its 400-acre private nature reserve offering an array of activities including birdwatching, horseback riding, and guided tours of Maya archaeological sites. The resort's focus on conservation and community involvement creates a uniquely immersive experience for guests, who can also enjoy amenities such as the hilltop spa and farm-to-table dining. For bookings, visit https://www.chaacreek.com/.

Matachica Resort & Spa

Located on the tranquil shores of Ambergris Caye, Matachica Resort & Spa offers a secluded boutique hotel experience with a focus on luxury and relaxation. Rooms begin at approximately $400 per night, with accommodations that include private casitas and beachfront villas, each designed with vibrant Caribbean decor and modern amenities. Matachica is a haven for those seeking tranquility, offering a spa with treatments inspired by the surrounding natural beauty, as well as an infinity pool overlooking the ocean. Guests can dine at the award-winning Mambo Restaurant, which serves locally sourced, gourmet cuisine in an intimate, candlelit setting. For bookings, visit https://www.matachica.com/

2.6 Unique Stays: Eco-Lodges and Island Resorts

The eco-lodges and island resorts scattered across the country offer a unique blend of sustainability, comfort, and authentic experiences. These accommodations provide guests with the opportunity to enjoy the unspoiled beauty of Belize while staying in environmentally-conscious lodgings that respect the natural world. From rustic jungle retreats to private island hideaways, Belize's eco-lodges and island resorts promise an unforgettable stay, immersing visitors in the serenity and wonders of this Caribbean paradise.

Chan Chich Lodge

Located deep in the rainforests of northwestern Belize, Chan Chich Lodge offers a one-of-a-kind experience for nature lovers and adventure seekers. Set within a 130,000-acre private nature reserve, the lodge is surrounded by ancient Maya ruins and an abundance of wildlife, including jaguars, howler monkeys, and exotic birds. Lodging prices start at around $450 per night, and guests stay in thatched-roof cabanas that blend seamlessly into the jungle surroundings. The lodge's amenities include guided wildlife tours, a swimming pool, and an open-air restaurant serving farm-to-table cuisine. Chan Chich's commitment to conservation and sustainable tourism makes it a top choice for eco-conscious travelers looking to reconnect with nature. To make reservations, visit https://chanchich.com/.

Belcampo Lodge
Belcampo Lodge, located in the southern region of Belize near Punta Gorda, offers a luxurious eco-lodge experience that celebrates both nature and Belizean culture. The lodge, which focuses on sustainability and responsible tourism, is set on a vast organic farm and rainforest reserve. Guests stay in spacious jungle suites starting at $400 per night, each featuring outdoor showers, private verandas, and breathtaking views of the surrounding wilderness. Belcampo's unique offerings include farm-to-table dining, guided nature hikes, chocolate-making workshops, and river kayaking. The lodge's eco-conscious philosophy and its emphasis on sustainability make it a perfect retreat for those who value luxury with a minimal environmental footprint. To make reservations, visit https://belcampo-lodge.hotels-belize.com/.

Hamanasi Adventure and Dive Resort
Located in Hopkins, Hamanasi Adventure and Dive Resort offers the rare combination of access to both Belize's stunning coral reefs and its lush rainforests. This eco-friendly resort provides guests with a variety of accommodations, from beachfront rooms to private treehouse suites. Prices start at approximately $350 per night, with all-inclusive packages available that cover meals, tours, and diving excursions. The resort offers a wide array of eco-adventures, including reef diving, rainforest treks, and exploring ancient Maya ruins. Hamanasi's dedication to sustainability is evident in its environmental initiatives, including its rainwater harvesting system and its support of local conservation efforts. It's the perfect destination for travelers looking to experience the best of both Belize's underwater and terrestrial ecosystems. To make reservations, visit https://www.hamanasi.com/.

Thatch Caye Resort
For travelers seeking a laid-back, island-vibe experience, Thatch Caye Resort is an ideal choice. Located on a private island within the Belize Barrier Reef, this

eco-resort offers over-water bungalows and island cabanas starting at $400 per night. Guests can unwind in the island's peaceful, car-free environment, where palm trees, sandy beaches, and clear waters set the scene for ultimate relaxation. The resort offers activities such as snorkeling, paddleboarding, and fly-fishing, while its eco-friendly design ensures minimal impact on the surrounding environment. Thatch Caye's all-inclusive packages cover meals, activities, and airport transfers, allowing guests to enjoy a carefree stay in paradise. The resort's commitment to sustainability, combined with its stunning location, makes it an unforgettable choice for a unique island escape. To make reservations, visit https://thatchcayebelize.com/.

Lamanai Outpost Lodge
Situated on the banks of the New River Lagoon and surrounded by the Maya ruins of Lamanai, the Lamanai Outpost Lodge offers a truly unique stay that combines history, culture, and nature. This eco-lodge is renowned for its intimate setting and expert-guided tours, which take guests through the rainforest, wetlands, and ancient ruins. The rustic cabanas, priced around $200 per night, are designed to blend into the surrounding jungle while providing all the necessary comforts. Guests can enjoy bird-watching, crocodile-spotting tours, and night excursions to witness the incredible wildlife. The lodge's remote location and focus on conservation and eco-tourism make it a favorite among travelers looking to experience Belize's rich cultural heritage and biodiversity. To make reservations, visit https://lamanai.com/.

CHAPTER 3
TRANSPORTATION

3.1 Getting Around Belize

Belize is a small yet diverse country, where navigating through its unique regions can offer a truly enriching experience. Getting around Belize is a relatively straightforward experience, thanks to the country's well-connected transport network. For those traveling within the city or exploring the islands and jungles, buses and taxis are the primary modes of transportation. Buses operate frequently between towns and are an affordable option for both locals and visitors. Taxis are widely available in urban areas, and while meters are not always used, negotiating a fair price in advance ensures a smooth ride. For visitors who wish to explore at their own pace, renting a car is a convenient choice. Belize's roads, while generally well-maintained, can vary in quality, especially in rural areas. A 4x4 vehicle might be necessary for some off-the-beaten-path locations, particularly during the rainy season when roads can become tricky to navigate. Gas stations are scattered throughout the country, though it's advisable to refuel in major towns before heading into more remote areas.

Water taxis provide a unique way of getting around the coastal regions and islands. These boats shuttle passengers between Belize City and popular island destinations such as Caye Caulker and Ambergris Caye. The trips are relatively inexpensive and offer a scenic way to travel, providing stunning views of the Caribbean Sea. Ferries run frequently, making it easy to hop between islands, and tickets can be purchased online or at the docks. For short-haul flights within Belize, domestic airlines like Maya Island Air and Tropic Air offer regular services. These small planes operate from the main international airport in Belize City to smaller towns such as San Pedro, Placencia, and Punta Gorda. Flights are quick and offer incredible aerial views of the country's diverse landscapes. While pricier than other transport options, flying is the fastest way to reach more remote destinations. Cycling is also a popular way to explore the towns and coastal regions, particularly for travelers seeking an eco-friendly option. Many guesthouses and hotels offer bicycle rentals, and the flat terrain makes it easy to pedal through charming streets and along beautiful beaches.

3.2 Public Transportation Options

Exploring Belize is a vibrant experience, rich with diverse landscapes and cultures, and understanding the public transport options available can significantly enhance this journey. The country's transportation network is designed to cater to both locals and visitors, making it relatively easy to navigate its charming towns, bustling markets, and breathtaking natural attractions. From colorful buses to water taxis, each mode of transport offers a unique glimpse into the daily lives of Belizeans, while also providing practical means for travelers to reach their desired destinations.

Buses

One of the most common forms of public transport in Belize is the bus system, often referred to as "chicken buses." These brightly painted vehicles are converted school buses, and they serve as an affordable and essential means of travel throughout the country. The prices for bus rides are typically modest, ranging from $2 to $15 depending on the distance. For instance, a ride from Belize City to San Ignacio might cost around $7, while longer trips, like those to Placencia, could be slightly higher. Buses depart from various terminals and roadside stops, and although they might not run on a strict schedule, they generally follow set routes. Travelers should be prepared for a lively atmosphere onboard, as these buses often become communal spaces filled with laughter, music, and the aroma of local snacks.

Water Taxis

For those wishing to explore the coastal regions or the picturesque islands, water taxis are an excellent option. These boats provide essential connections between Belize City and destinations like Caye Caulker and Ambergris Caye. Prices for water taxi rides vary based on the destination, generally costing between $15 and $25 for a one-way trip. Tickets can be purchased at designated terminals in Belize City or directly from the boat operators. The journey by water taxi not only provides an efficient means of transportation but also offers breathtaking views of the Caribbean Sea and a refreshing sea breeze. It's advisable to check the schedule in advance, as the frequency of boats can vary throughout the day, especially during off-peak seasons.

Taxis and Ride-Sharing Services

While buses and water taxis are prevalent, taxis also play a significant role in public transport within cities and towns. Unlike metered taxis in many countries,

Belizean taxis typically operate on a flat-rate system based on the destination. Fares are negotiable, and it's wise for visitors to agree on a price before embarking on their journey. Taxis are readily available in major towns and at airports, providing convenience for those traveling with luggage or in larger groups. Additionally, ride-sharing services have begun to emerge, allowing for greater flexibility in transportation choices. Apps like Uber are not yet widespread, but local alternatives may provide similar services in more urban areas, offering an efficient way to get around.

Shuttle Services

For travelers seeking a more comfortable and direct option, shuttle services are a popular choice. These services operate between major tourist destinations and often include pickup and drop-off at hotels. Prices for shuttle rides can range from $25 to $50 per person, depending on the distance and whether the service is private or shared. Shuttle companies typically require advance bookings, which can be made online or through hotel concierges. These vehicles provide a more personal experience, often accommodating smaller groups and offering additional amenities such as air conditioning and refreshments. This option is particularly appealing for those who wish to avoid the hustle and bustle of public buses while still enjoying the beautiful scenery along the way.

Tips for Using Public Transport in Belize

Navigating Belize's public transport system can be an adventure in itself, and understanding a few key tips can enhance the experience. It's advisable for visitors to have some local currency on hand, as many services may not accept credit cards. Knowing a few basic phrases in English or Spanish can also be helpful, particularly when asking for directions or negotiating taxi fares. Additionally, keeping an eye on personal belongings while traveling is essential, as crowded buses and busy terminals can be hotspots for petty theft. Engaging with locals can provide valuable insights and tips about the best routes, hidden gems, and local customs, adding depth to the journey.

3.3 Car Rentals and Driving Tips

Renting a car in Belize offers a level of freedom and flexibility that can transform a trip into an unforgettable adventure. With its diverse landscapes, from tropical rainforests to pristine beaches, having a personal vehicle allows visitors to explore Belize's hidden gems at their own pace. Car rental services are widely available throughout Belize, especially in popular tourist areas and major cities like Belize City, San Ignacio, and Placencia. A variety of companies cater to different budgets and needs, offering everything from compact cars to rugged SUVs suited for off-road adventures. Prices for car rentals typically range from $50 to $100 per day, depending on the type of vehicle and the rental duration. It's recommended to book in advance, particularly during peak tourist seasons, to secure the best rates and vehicle availability. Additionally, many companies offer airport pickup services, which is convenient for travelers arriving in Belize by air.

Top Car Rental Companies in Belize

Crystal Auto Rental
One well-known company is Crystal Auto Rental, located in Belize City with a convenient office near Philip S.W. Goldson International Airport. Crystal Auto Rental is popular for its wide range of vehicles, from sedans to 4x4 SUVs, making it ideal for travelers planning to explore rural areas. The company offers competitive pricing, with rates typically starting at $55 per day. Their commitment to customer service and vehicle maintenance makes them a reliable choice for visitors. You can book through their website at https://www.crystalautorentalbelize.com/.

Avis Belize
Another reputable option is Avis Belize, also situated near the international airport in Belize City. As part of a global brand, Avis ensures high service standards and provides a fleet that includes economy cars and SUVs. This well-established company is known for its professionalism and efficient booking processes, making it a convenient choice for travelers looking for quality and reliability during their stay in Belize. For reservations, visit their website at https://www.avis.com/en/locations/bz.

Matus Car Rental
In San Ignacio, Matus Car Rental stands out as a trusted local provider, offering rental options starting around $60 per day. Known for its personalized service and local expertise, Matus Car Rental is perfect for visitors wanting to explore nearby attractions such as the Xunantunich ruins and the Mountain Pine Ridge Forest Reserve. Their fleet includes various vehicles tailored to meet the needs of adventure-seekers and casual travelers alike.

Budget Belize
Budget Belize offers another excellent choice for budget-conscious travelers, with rates starting at $50 per day. Located in Belize City, this company focuses on providing affordable rental options without sacrificing quality. Their straightforward booking process and customer service make it an attractive option for those seeking a reliable vehicle to navigate Belize's attractions and scenic landscapes. You can explore their offerings at https://www.budget-belize.com/.

Barefoot Services
For those traveling to Placencia, Barefoot Services provides well-maintained vehicles at around $70 per day. Known for their friendly customer service and attention to detail, Barefoot Services ensures a seamless rental experience for visitors looking to explore the southern regions of Belize. Their diverse fleet, coupled with local knowledge, enhances the adventure for travelers heading to this picturesque beach town. Book your vehicle through their website at https://barefootservicesbelize.com/.

Jabiru Auto Rentals
Meanwhile, Jabiru Auto Rentals serves visitors arriving from Mexico with affordable options starting at $55 per day. Located in Corozal, this locally-owned business caters to travelers venturing into northern Belize. Jabiru Auto Rentals prides itself on providing a selection of vehicles suited for various terrains, ensuring visitors can explore the region's natural beauty comfortably.

Driving in Belize
Driving in Belize can be a pleasant experience, provided visitors are aware of the country's driving conditions and regulations. Major highways like the George Price and Hummingbird Highways are well-maintained, but rural roads can be unpaved and challenging. It's essential to rent a four-wheel-drive vehicle if planning to explore more remote areas. Speed limits are generally 25 miles per hour in towns and 55 miles per hour on highways. Driving is on the right side of the road, and road signs are in English, making it easy for international visitors to navigate.

Required Documentation and Age Restrictions
When renting a car, international visitors need to present a valid driver's license from their home country. Most companies do not require an international driving

permit, but it's always a good idea to confirm this with the rental agency beforehand. The typical minimum age for renting a vehicle in Belize is 25, although some companies may allow younger drivers for an additional fee. Before setting off, ensure the car is thoroughly inspected for any damage and documented to avoid misunderstandings upon returning the vehicle.

Fuel and Roadside Assistance

Fuel stations are available along major routes and in larger towns, although it's wise to refuel in larger areas before heading into rural regions. Gas prices are typically higher than in North America, and while most stations accept both cash and credit cards, some smaller stations may prefer local currency. Many rental companies, such as Crystal Auto Rental and Budget Belize, provide roadside assistance as part of their rental packages. Make sure to carry the company's emergency contact number in case you need assistance during your travels.

Parking and Safety Considerations

Parking in Belize is generally straightforward, especially outside of larger towns. Hotels and tourist attractions often provide free parking, but it's essential to inquire beforehand. In busy areas like Belize City and San Pedro, parking may be more limited, especially during peak hours. Visitors should avoid leaving valuables visible in the car and take standard safety precautions such as locking the vehicle and parking in well-lit areas. While Belize is generally safe for tourists, being vigilant ensures a trouble-free experience.

3.4 Water Taxis and Boat Tours

Exploring Belize by water opens up a world of adventure and beauty. The country's stunning coastline and nearby cayes make water taxis and boat tours a vital part of the visitor experience. With crystal-clear waters, rich marine life, and breathtaking views, these trips offer a unique way to connect with Belize's natural treasures. Whether you're heading to the idyllic islands or cruising along Belize's rivers, the water journey is often as captivating as the destination itself.

Belize Express Water Taxi

The Belize Express Water Taxi offers a scenic and efficient connection between Belize City and the northern cayes. With regular departures to Caye Caulker and Ambergris Caye, the ride gives travelers a chance to breathe in the fresh Caribbean air while watching the sparkling waters. As you approach the islands, the view of palm-fringed shores and colorful local life immediately puts you in vacation mode. Prices are affordable, and their sleek boats make for a smooth and comfortable journey. This is more than just transport—it's the start of an unforgettable island adventure.

San Pedro Belize Express
San Pedro Belize Express Water Taxi is a reliable service for travelers seeking to visit Ambergris Caye and Caye Caulker. Departing from Belize City, this water taxi glides across the Caribbean Sea, providing passengers with stunning views of the surrounding turquoise waters. As the boat cuts through the waves, anticipation builds for the white sandy beaches and vibrant island life awaiting you. The ride is fast, efficient, and allows you to fully immerse yourself in Belize's tropical environment. This is the ideal way to travel for those wanting to experience the islands at their own pace.

Ocean Ferry Belize
Ocean Ferry Belize offers another comfortable option for travelers looking to explore the northern cayes. Their water taxis depart frequently from Belize City, offering a reliable service to destinations like Caye Caulker and San Pedro. As the boat speeds along, you can enjoy panoramic views of the Belize Barrier Reef in the distance, a reminder of the rich biodiversity hidden beneath the surface. The journey itself is an invitation to experience Belize's unparalleled marine beauty, whether you're heading for a dive or simply to relax by the beach.

Coral Tours Boat Service
Coral Tours specializes in personalized boat tours that take visitors to Belize's most stunning marine locations. Their tours provide access to lesser-known islands and snorkeling spots, where you can witness vibrant coral reefs and diverse sea life. These small-group tours allow for a more intimate experience, ensuring you get close to the beauty of Belize's underwater world. The knowledgeable guides enhance the journey, offering insights into the ecology and history of the region. For those seeking adventure and discovery, Coral Tours offers a memorable way to connect with Belize's marine treasures.

Thunderbolt Water Taxi
The Thunderbolt Water Taxi service connects the northern town of Corozal with San Pedro, making it a convenient choice for travelers looking to explore the northern coast. Known for its fast service, Thunderbolt taxis slice through the

calm waters of the Caribbean, giving passengers a breezy and scenic trip. As you leave the mainland behind, the boat journey transitions from town life to the laid-back island atmosphere. It's a journey filled with anticipation, as the open sea and clear skies guide you toward the sandy beaches of Ambergris Caye.

3.5 Domestic Flights and Air Services

While road and sea transport provide scenic ways to navigate the country, domestic flights offer an unparalleled level of convenience and speed, connecting remote and often inaccessible locations. With Belize's numerous islands, pristine jungles, and spread-out communities, air travel becomes essential for visitors who wish to make the most of their time. These domestic flights operate efficiently, offering reliable services that allow travelers to experience the country from a unique vantage point. Whether flying over the sparkling waters of the Caribbean or the dense green canopy of the rainforest, these flights provide more than just transportation—they deliver a remarkable aerial introduction to the beauty of Belize.

Tropic Air

Tropic Air is one of the most prominent and trusted air service providers in Belize. Operating since 1979, Tropic Air has grown into the largest airline in the country, connecting key destinations such as Belize City, San Pedro, Caye Caulker, Dangriga, and Placencia. With hubs at both the Philip S.W. Goldson International Airport and the Municipal Airport in Belize City, Tropic Air offers frequent flights to these popular tourist spots. Prices for flights can vary depending on the destination, with short flights like those to San Pedro costing around $80 one way. One of Tropic Air's unique features is the panoramic views provided by their small aircraft, allowing passengers to witness Belize's breathtaking coastline and reefs from above. Their commitment to safety and customer service, combined with scenic flights, makes Tropic Air a top choice for domestic travel.

Maya Island Air

Maya Island Air is another highly reputable domestic airline in Belize, offering an extensive network of flights across the country. Based in Belize City, with its main hub at the Municipal Airport, Maya Island Air connects popular tourist destinations such as Caye Caulker, San Pedro, Corozal, and Placencia. The airline is known for its reliability and efficient services, ensuring that travelers can move quickly between the mainland and Belize's beautiful cayes. Prices for flights to nearby islands typically range from $75 to $100, depending on the destination. What sets Maya Island Air apart is its focus on personalized customer care, ensuring that passengers enjoy a smooth and comfortable journey. Their aircraft are well-maintained, and the short flight durations allow travelers to spend more time enjoying their destinations.

Astrum Helicopters
Astrum Helicopters offers a unique air travel experience, providing both domestic flights and scenic tours throughout Belize. Based in Belize City, Astrum specializes in helicopter transfers that allow passengers to reach remote locations such as private islands, jungle lodges, and archaeological sites. While more expensive than traditional airlines, with prices starting around $300 per flight, the experience is unparalleled. Astrum Helicopters offers a bird's-eye view of Belize's most spectacular landscapes, from the Blue Hole to the Mayan ruins. This is the perfect option for travelers looking for luxury, exclusivity, and an unforgettable journey through the skies of Belize. Their helicopters are equipped with large windows, providing passengers with exceptional views throughout the flight.

Tropic Air Charter Services
In addition to their regular scheduled flights, Tropic Air also offers charter services that allow travelers to customize their journeys. Whether flying to remote islands, private resorts, or less-traveled parts of Belize, Tropic Air Charter provides flexibility and convenience. Charter flights are priced based on distance and aircraft type, typically starting at $500 for short flights. One of the standout features of Tropic Air's charter services is the ability to fly directly to destinations that are not served by regular routes. This service is ideal for groups, families, or those seeking privacy, allowing for a tailored experience without the constraints of flight schedules. The charter planes also provide the same stunning aerial views that Tropic Air is known for, ensuring that the journey is as memorable as the destination.

Maya Island Air Charter Flights
Maya Island Air also offers charter services for travelers seeking customized air travel in Belize. With a strong presence at both international and municipal airports, Maya Island Air Charter is ideal for visitors wanting to explore Belize's more remote or off-the-beaten-path locations. Prices for charter services vary based on the distance and size of the aircraft, typically starting at around $600.

Maya Island Air's fleet includes small planes that can land on short runways, providing access to destinations like private islands, nature reserves, and jungle lodges. The flexibility of chartering a flight means that travelers can create their own itinerary, maximizing their time and experience in Belize. With experienced pilots and well-maintained aircraft, Maya Island Air ensures both safety and a high level of comfort throughout the journey.

Blue Sky Aviation
Blue Sky Aviation offers another option for domestic air travel in Belize, specializing in small, private charters that cater to both locals and tourists. Based out of Belize City, Blue Sky provides services to various locations, including Punta Gorda, Hopkins, and even custom routes to private locations. Prices for these charters typically start around $450, depending on the route and aircraft size. What makes Blue Sky Aviation stand out is its commitment to providing personalized service, focusing on the individual needs of each client. The small, intimate aircraft allow for a relaxed and private travel experience, ideal for those looking to avoid crowded commercial flights. With experienced pilots and scenic routes, Blue Sky Aviation offers a unique way to see Belize's stunning landscapes from above.

CHAPTER 4
TOP 10 ATTRACTIONS & HIDDEN GEMS

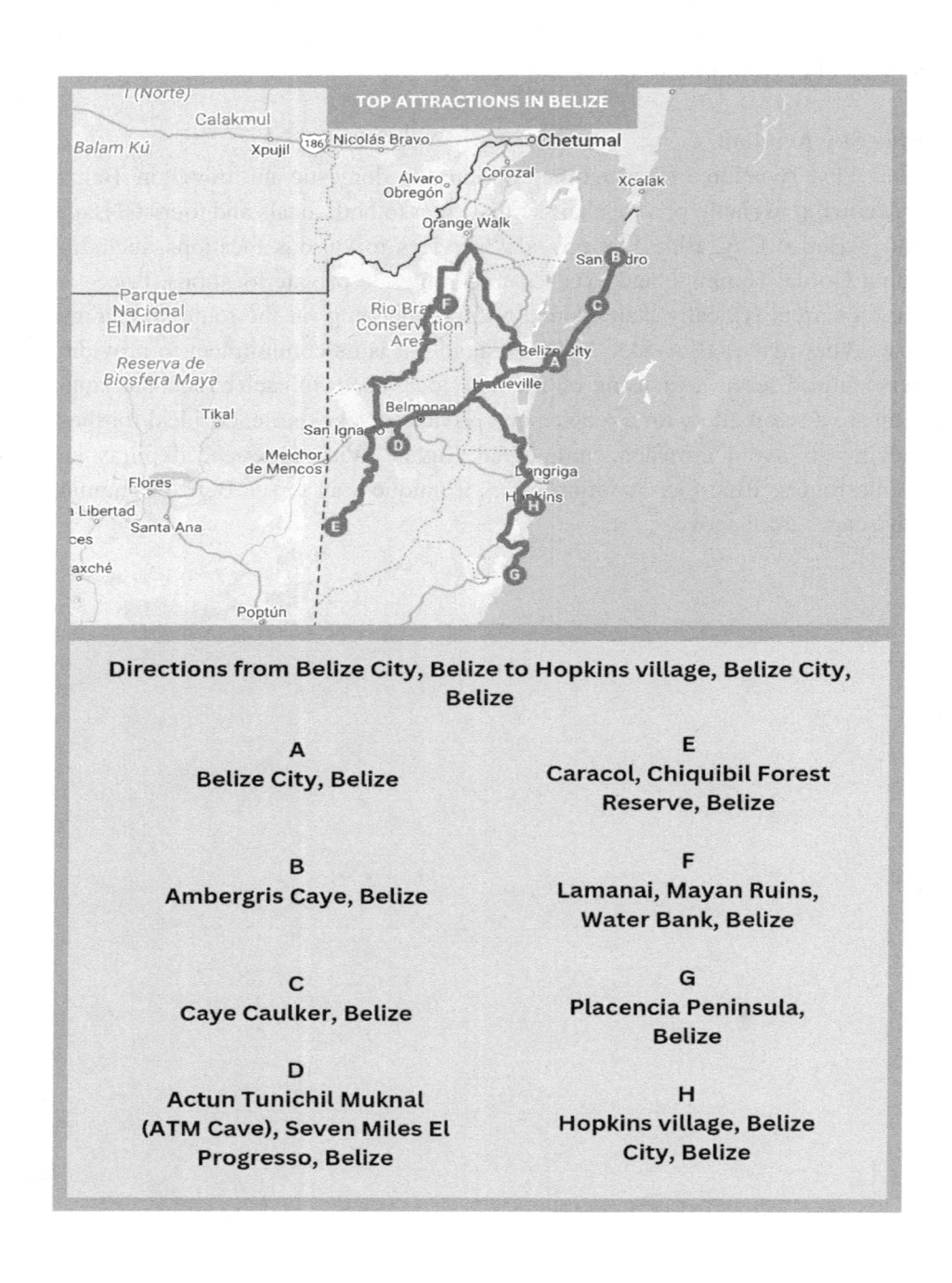

TOP ATTRACTIONS IN BELIZE

Directions from Belize City, Belize to Hopkins village, Belize City, Belize

A
Belize City, Belize

B
Ambergris Caye, Belize

C
Caye Caulker, Belize

D
Actun Tunichil Muknal (ATM Cave), Seven Miles El Progresso, Belize

E
Caracol, Chiquibil Forest Reserve, Belize

F
Lamanai, Mayan Ruins, Water Bank, Belize

G
Placencia Peninsula, Belize

H
Hopkins village, Belize City, Belize

4.1 Belize Barrier Reef

The Belize Barrier Reef, a UNESCO World Heritage Site, is one of Belize's most stunning natural attractions. Located along the coast, this vast reef system stretches over 300 kilometers, offering an underwater paradise. It's the second-largest coral reef in the world, only after Australia's Great Barrier Reef. The reef's vibrant coral, diverse marine life, and pristine waters make it a must-visit for nature lovers. It is a haven for snorkelers, divers, and anyone looking to explore a world beneath the waves.

Getting to the Belize Barrier Reef
Reaching the Belize Barrier Reef is a simple and scenic adventure. Visitors can access the reef via boat tours departing from popular spots like Caye Caulker, Ambergris Caye, and Placencia. Many of the islands and cayes along the reef are just a short boat ride away from the mainland. With numerous tour operators available, arranging a trip to this underwater marvel is both easy and accessible. Whether staying on the islands or the mainland, the reef's wonders are always within reach.

Entry Fees and Accessibility
Access to the Belize Barrier Reef generally comes through organized tours, many of which include an entry fee to marine reserves. The entry fee usually ranges from $10 to $15, depending on the area of the reef. This fee goes towards

conservation efforts to protect the fragile ecosystem. Most areas of the reef are accessible year-round, offering opportunities to explore its vibrant marine life and crystal-clear waters. The experience is not only immersive but also supports the preservation of Belize's precious natural heritage.

Why It's Worth Visiting
The Belize Barrier Reef is worth visiting for its breathtaking beauty and unparalleled biodiversity. With over 500 species of fish, 100 species of coral, and countless other marine creatures, the reef is a living masterpiece. Its vibrant underwater world offers a unique opportunity to witness marine ecosystems in their most natural state. The coral formations and aquatic life create a stunning underwater landscape that cannot be found anywhere else in the world. For those seeking a transformative experience, the reef delivers a glimpse into one of nature's greatest treasures.

Historical and Cultural Significance
The Belize Barrier Reef holds deep historical and cultural significance for Belizeans. For centuries, the reef has sustained local communities by providing fish and protecting the coastline from storms. It has also played an important role in Belize's tourism industry, attracting visitors from around the world. Beyond its natural importance, the reef symbolizes Belize's commitment to conservation and environmental stewardship. This legacy makes a visit to the reef not just an adventure but also a connection to the country's rich cultural heritage.

Activities and What to Do
The Belize Barrier Reef offers a wealth of activities for every type of visitor. Snorkeling and scuba diving are the most popular ways to explore the vibrant marine life and colorful coral formations. Visitors can swim alongside nurse sharks, stingrays, and even sea turtles in crystal-clear waters. For those seeking a more relaxed experience, boat tours provide an above-water view of the reef's beauty. No matter how you choose to explore, the reef promises an unforgettable experience with nature at its finest.

Other Information a Visitor Needs to Know
Visitors to the Belize Barrier Reef should plan their trips during the dry season, from November to April, for the best conditions. Many tour operators offer half-day or full-day excursions, providing all necessary gear and guided

experiences. It's essential to follow local guidelines for protecting the reef, such as avoiding touching coral or disturbing marine life. With its stunning underwater landscapes and thriving biodiversity, the Belize Barrier Reef offers an unforgettable adventure that will leave every traveler inspired.

4.2 Blue Hole

The Great Blue Hole is one of the most iconic and breathtaking attractions in Belize. Located off the coast of Belize, this natural marvel is a massive underwater sinkhole within the Lighthouse Reef Atoll. Its perfectly circular shape and deep blue color make it a unique geological formation visible from the air and sea. Measuring over 300 meters in diameter and about 125 meters deep, it attracts adventurers, divers, and explorers from around the globe.

How to Get to the Blue Hole
Reaching the Blue Hole requires a boat ride from Belize City or nearby cayes like Caye Caulker and Ambergris Caye. Most tours are full-day excursions and include stops at nearby reefs and islands. Helicopter tours are also available for those wanting an aerial view of the Blue Hole's stunning symmetry. Both options offer incredible ways to experience this natural wonder, with boat tours offering the chance to dive or snorkel in its deep waters.

Entry Fees and Accessibility
The entry fee for the Great Blue Hole is approximately $40 per person, which supports conservation efforts within the marine reserve. Most tour operators include this fee in their packages, making it convenient for visitors. The Blue Hole is accessible year-round, but the best time to visit is during the dry season, when waters are calm and visibility is optimal. For those venturing below the surface, scuba diving and snorkeling tours are the primary ways to experience the magic of this underwater world.

Why It's Worth Visiting
The Blue Hole is worth visiting for its extraordinary beauty and world-renowned diving opportunities. Its deep waters are home to stalactites, unique rock formations, and rare species of fish and marine life. The sense of descending into an ancient, untouched realm is both thrilling and awe-inspiring. Whether from above or below, the Blue Hole's stunning natural symmetry makes it an unparalleled experience that promises to leave visitors in awe of nature's power and creativity.

Historical and Cultural Significance
The Great Blue Hole is not only a natural marvel but also a piece of Earth's geological history. Formed thousands of years ago during the last Ice Age, the sinkhole reveals layers of the Earth's development. Famous ocean explorer Jacques Cousteau named it one of the top five diving sites in the world, cementing its place in diving lore. The Blue Hole also plays a vital role in Belize's marine ecosystem, contributing to the region's rich biodiversity and environmental heritage.

Activities and What to Do
Visitors to the Blue Hole can enjoy some of the best diving and snorkeling experiences in the world. Scuba diving offers an opportunity to explore its depths, marveling at the rock formations and underwater caverns. For snorkelers, the shallow waters around the rim offer a chance to swim alongside reef sharks, fish, and coral species. Beyond diving, helicopter tours provide a stunning aerial view of the Blue Hole's perfect circular shape and its contrast with the surrounding turquoise waters.

Other Information a Visitor Needs to Know
When planning a visit to the Blue Hole, it's essential to book tours in advance, especially during peak season. The trip to the Blue Hole can take two to three hours by boat, so visitors should be prepared for a full-day adventure. Scuba diving trips generally require certification due to the depth of the dive, but snorkeling tours are available for all skill levels. As one of the world's most remarkable natural wonders, the Great Blue Hole promises an unforgettable adventure in the heart of Belize's stunning marine landscape.

4.3 Ambergris Caye

Ambergris Caye, Belize's largest island, is a true paradise tucked away in the Caribbean. Located just off the coast of northern Belize, this island offers stunning beaches and vibrant marine life. Visitors will find a peaceful yet lively atmosphere, making it perfect for both relaxation and adventure. Whether you're snorkeling the reef or soaking up the sun, Ambergris Caye offers an unmatched island escape.

Getting to Ambergris Caye
Reaching Ambergris Caye is a simple journey from Belize City. Visitors can take a quick 15-minute flight from the city or opt for a scenic water taxi ride that takes about 90 minutes. Flights are offered daily by local airlines, and water taxis depart regularly from the mainland. Upon arrival, visitors are greeted with the island's laid-back charm and breathtaking coastal views. Both options offer a picturesque introduction to this beautiful island.

Entry Fees and Accessibility
Ambergris Caye itself does not require an entry fee, making it an accessible destination for all. Visitors can explore the island freely, with plenty of beaches and nature to enjoy without additional costs. However, some specific attractions, like marine reserves or guided tours, may have fees that go towards conservation. The island is welcoming year-round, with easy access to beaches,

local shops, and restaurants. This accessibility makes Ambergris Caye an inviting stop for travelers of all kinds.

Why It's Worth Visiting
Ambergris Caye is worth visiting for its perfect blend of relaxation and adventure. Its proximity to the Belize Barrier Reef offers incredible opportunities for diving and snorkeling in some of the world's clearest waters. The island's charm lies in its peaceful atmosphere, where visitors can explore vibrant coral reefs by day and enjoy beachside dining by night. From swimming with colorful marine life to lounging under palm trees, Ambergris Caye offers something for everyone. The natural beauty and warmth of the island create an unforgettable experience.

Historical and Cultural Significance
Ambergris Caye has a rich history, with roots stretching back to the Maya civilization, who once used the island as a trading post. Today, the island reflects a blend of local cultures, including Creole, Maya, and Mestizo influences. Its fishing community remains vital, with locals still relying on the sea for their livelihoods. This deep connection to the ocean shapes the island's culture, making it a place where tradition and nature coexist beautifully. Ambergris Caye offers visitors a glimpse into Belize's past, while embracing its vibrant present.

Activities and What to Do
Ambergris Caye is a hub of activity, offering countless ways to enjoy its natural beauty. Visitors can snorkel or dive at the famous Hol Chan Marine Reserve or Shark Ray Alley, where marine life thrives. For those seeking relaxation, the island's beaches provide the perfect backdrop for a day of lounging. Kayaking, paddleboarding, and sailing are also popular, giving visitors a chance to explore the island's waters from different perspectives. Whether in the sea or on land, Ambergris Caye is full of opportunities for adventure and discovery.

Other Information a Visitor Needs to Know
Visitors should plan their trip to Ambergris Caye between November and April for the best weather. Golf carts are the main mode of transport on the island, available for rent upon arrival. The island has a variety of accommodations, from luxurious resorts to charming beachfront cottages, catering to all budgets. Ambergris Caye's friendly locals and welcoming atmosphere ensure that every

traveler feels at home. Whether exploring the reef or enjoying a sunset on the beach, this hidden gem promises an unforgettable Belizean experience.

4.4 Caye Caulker

Caye Caulker, a charming island just off the coast of Belize, offers an enchanting escape for travelers seeking a laid-back atmosphere. Located about 21 miles from Belize City, this small island is renowned for its stunning beaches, vibrant marine life, and welcoming community. With a motto of "Go Slow," Caye Caulker invites visitors to unwind and immerse themselves in the natural beauty of the Caribbean.

Getting There
Reaching Caye Caulker is a delightful journey in itself. Visitors can take a water taxi or a small plane from Belize City, with water taxis providing regular service throughout the day. The boat ride typically takes about 45 minutes, offering picturesque views of the turquoise waters and surrounding cayes. For those preferring a bird's-eye view, flights via local airlines like Tropic Air or Maya Island Air make the journey in just 15 minutes, making it accessible for everyone.

Entry Fees and Accessibility

There are no entry fees to Caye Caulker itself, making it an affordable destination for all travelers. The island is pedestrian-friendly, encouraging exploration on foot or by bicycle. Many accommodations, restaurants, and attractions are within easy walking distance, allowing visitors to soak in the island's vibrant atmosphere at their own pace. This accessibility enhances the island's charm, inviting guests to experience the local culture fully.

Why It's Worth Visiting

Caye Caulker is worth a visit for its stunning natural beauty and relaxed vibe. The island is surrounded by the Belize Barrier Reef, offering unparalleled snorkeling and diving opportunities just a short boat ride away. Visitors are captivated by the crystal-clear waters, swaying palm trees, and soft sandy beaches that create an idyllic tropical paradise. The friendly atmosphere and sense of community make every traveler feel welcomed, fostering an unforgettable experience.

Historical and Cultural Significance

Caye Caulker has a rich history that reflects the diverse cultures of Belize. Originally inhabited by the Maya, the island has also seen influences from the British and Creole communities. Today, it is a blend of cultures, evident in the local cuisine, music, and festivals. The island's fishing heritage remains vital, with lobster and conch being key components of the local diet. Visiting Caye Caulker offers a glimpse into this vibrant cultural tapestry, connecting travelers to the island's past.

Activities and What to Do

Caye Caulker is a haven for outdoor enthusiasts, offering an array of activities to suit every interest. Snorkeling and diving are top attractions, with nearby spots like the Hol Chan Marine Reserve and Shark Ray Alley teeming with marine life. Visitors can also rent bicycles or golf carts to explore the island at leisure, or simply relax on the beach with a good book. Sunset sailing tours provide a magical end to the day, as the sun dips below the horizon, painting the sky in brilliant hues.

Culinary Delights and Local Cuisine

Culinary experiences in Caye Caulker are a treat for the senses, with many local eateries serving fresh seafood and traditional Belizean dishes. The island's famous "lobster fest" celebrates the local catch, allowing visitors to savor dishes prepared in various mouth-watering styles. Dining at a beachside restaurant while enjoying the ocean breeze adds to the island's charm, making meals an integral part of the experience.

Accommodations and Local Hospitality
Caye Caulker offers a range of accommodations, from budget-friendly hostels to charming beachfront hotels. Many establishments reflect the island's laid-back vibe, with friendly staff eager to assist and provide insider tips on the best local experiences. Staying on the island allows visitors to fully embrace the slower pace of life and immerse themselves in the welcoming community atmosphere.

4.5 Actun Tunichil Muknal (ATM) Cave

Actun Tunichil Muknal, often referred to as ATM Cave, is one of Belize's most awe-inspiring hidden gems, offering a unique blend of natural beauty and rich cultural history. Located in the heart of the Belizean jungle, near the village of San Ignacio, this cave is not only a stunning geological formation but also a significant archaeological site. Visitors are drawn to its intriguing history, breathtaking scenery, and the thrill of exploration, making it a must-see destination for adventurers.

Getting There

Reaching Actun Tunichil Muknal Cave involves a scenic journey through the lush landscapes of Belize. The cave is situated about 30 miles from San Ignacio, and most visitors opt for guided tours that include transportation. The journey typically involves a combination of driving and a short hike through the jungle, where travelers can immerse themselves in the vibrant flora and fauna of the region. This adventure provides an exhilarating prelude to the wonders that await inside the cave.

Entry Fees and Accessibility

To access ATM Cave, visitors must join a guided tour, which is mandatory for safety and preservation reasons. The entry fee generally ranges from $80 to $100 per person, which includes transportation, a guide, and equipment for exploring the cave. Tours often last around four to six hours, allowing ample time to experience the cave's beauty and history. This fee contributes to the maintenance of the site and the protection of its archaeological treasures, ensuring that future generations can enjoy its wonders.

Why It's Worth Visiting

Visiting Actun Tunichil Muknal Cave is an experience unlike any other, blending adventure with education. The cave is renowned for its stunning stalactites and stalagmites, creating a magical atmosphere that transports visitors to another world. What sets ATM Cave apart is its historical significance; it was used by the ancient Maya for ceremonial purposes, and the remains of sacrificial offerings can be found within. This unique combination of natural beauty and cultural history makes it a destination worth experiencing firsthand.

Historical and Cultural Significance

Actun Tunichil Muknal is a site of immense historical and cultural importance. The cave was a sacred space for the Maya, who believed it to be a gateway to the underworld. Archaeological findings include pottery, tools, and the remains of human sacrifices, all of which provide insight into ancient Maya rituals. The most famous discovery is the "Crystal Maiden," a skeleton adorned with calcite crystals, which serves as a powerful reminder of the cave's ceremonial significance. Exploring ATM Cave allows visitors to connect with the rich history of the Maya civilization in a profound way.

Activities and What to Do
Visitors to ATM Cave can engage in a variety of activities that enhance their experience. Guided tours typically involve a combination of hiking, swimming, and wading through shallow waters as you navigate the cave's passages. Inside, the cave reveals stunning geological formations, ancient artifacts, and fascinating wildlife. Photographers will find endless opportunities to capture the ethereal beauty of the cave, while history enthusiasts can delve into the stories of the Maya people and their reverence for this sacred site.

Safety and Preparation
To fully enjoy the experience at ATM Cave, visitors should come prepared for a physically demanding adventure. Comfortable, quick-drying clothing and sturdy water shoes are essential, as participants will be navigating wet and uneven terrain. Additionally, bringing a change of clothes for afterward is a smart choice, as you may get wet during the tour. Visitors should also follow the guide's instructions closely to ensure safety and respect for the cave's delicate ecosystem.

4.6 Caracol Mayan Ruins

Located deep in the jungles of Belize, the Caracol Mayan Ruins stand as a testament to the remarkable civilization that once flourished here. Located approximately 40 miles southwest of San Ignacio, Caracol is one of the largest and most significant archaeological sites in Belize, showcasing the grandeur of the ancient Maya. Often overlooked in favor of more famous sites, Caracol offers visitors a chance to explore a hidden gem steeped in history, culture, and natural beauty.

Getting There
Reaching Caracol involves a journey that adds to the allure of this hidden treasure. The site is best accessed by car, with a scenic drive through the lush rainforest along the Mountain Pine Ridge Road. Travelers can also join guided tours from San Ignacio, which often include transportation and a knowledgeable guide. The trip takes about two hours, allowing visitors to soak in the breathtaking landscapes of Belize before arriving at this ancient city.

Entry Fees and Accessibility
Visiting Caracol comes with a modest entry fee of around $10 per person, which helps maintain the site and support ongoing preservation efforts. The ruins are open daily, typically from 8 AM to 5 PM, allowing ample time for exploration. Once inside, visitors can roam freely among the impressive structures, experiencing the rich history of the Maya in an accessible and immersive environment. The site's layout encourages wandering, making it easy to lose oneself in the beauty and tranquility of the jungle.

Why It's Worth Visiting
Caracol is worth every moment spent exploring its grounds due to its remarkable architecture and historical significance. The site features over 35,000 structures, including temples, palaces, and plazas, all set against the backdrop of the verdant jungle. The highlight of Caracol is Caana, the tallest structure in Belize, which rises majestically to 143 feet and offers stunning panoramic views of the surrounding landscape. Visitors can appreciate the intricacy of the stone carvings and the engineering prowess of the ancient Maya, making it a captivating destination for history enthusiasts and nature lovers alike.

Historical and Cultural Significance
Dating back to around 1200 BC, Caracol was a thriving city during the Classic Period of Maya civilization. At its height, it is believed to have housed over 150,000 inhabitants and served as a significant political and economic center. The ruins reveal a wealth of information about the Maya's complex society, including their advanced agricultural practices, trade networks, and astronomical

knowledge. The cultural richness of Caracol provides a unique opportunity for visitors to connect with the legacy of the Maya, deepening their understanding of this fascinating civilization.

Activities and What to Do
Exploring Caracol is an adventure in itself, with plenty to see and do throughout the site. Visitors can climb the steep steps of Caana to enjoy breathtaking views, wander through the expansive plazas, and marvel at the intricate stone carvings adorning the buildings. Birdwatching is also a popular activity, as the surrounding jungle is home to numerous exotic species. Guided tours often include insights into the site's history, ecology, and the unique flora and fauna of the region, enriching the overall experience.

Guided Tours and Expert Insights
Engaging a knowledgeable guide is highly recommended for those wanting to fully appreciate the significance of Caracol. Many local tour companies offer guided trips that include transportation, lunch, and in-depth historical context about the ruins. These guides are invaluable, sharing fascinating stories and cultural insights that bring the ancient city to life. Their expertise allows visitors to gain a deeper understanding of the Maya civilization and the importance of Caracol within it.

Practical Information for Visitors
Travelers should consider bringing plenty of water, snacks, and sunscreen, as exploring Caracol can be both hot and tiring. Comfortable walking shoes are essential, as many of the pathways are uneven and can be challenging. It's also wise to bring a camera to capture the stunning vistas and intricate details of the ruins. For those looking to escape the crowds, visiting during the early morning or late afternoon can provide a more intimate experience with the ancient site.

4.7 Lamanai Mayan Ruins

Lamanai, a remarkable archaeological site, offers a captivating glimpse into the ancient Maya civilization. Located along the banks of the New River in northern Belize, this sprawling complex boasts a rich history dating back over three thousand years. Lamanai is not only known for its impressive temples and structures but also for its stunning natural surroundings, making it a must-visit for anyone intrigued by ancient cultures and breathtaking landscapes.

Location and Accessibility
Lamanai is situated approximately 20 miles from the town of Orange Walk, making it accessible by both land and water. The most common way to reach the ruins is via a scenic boat ride along the New River, which takes about 30 minutes and offers stunning views of the surrounding jungle and wildlife. Alternatively, visitors can opt for guided tours that combine transportation by land and boat, providing a comprehensive experience. The journey itself sets the stage for the adventure ahead, immersing travelers in Belize's lush environment.

Entry Fees and Visiting Hours
There is a nominal entry fee to visit Lamanai, typically around $10 per person, which helps support the site's maintenance and preservation. The site is open daily from 8 a.m. to 5 p.m., allowing ample time for exploration. Visitors are

encouraged to arrive early in the day to enjoy the cooler morning temperatures and to avoid crowds. The combination of reasonable entry fees and extended hours makes Lamanai an accessible destination for all types of travelers.

Why It's Worth Visiting
Lamanai is worth visiting for its breathtaking ruins and the stories they tell about the ancient Maya. The site is home to several impressive structures, including the Temple of the Jaguar Masks, the High Temple, and the Mask Temple, each adorned with intricate carvings that have withstood the test of time. Exploring these ruins offers an unparalleled opportunity to connect with history, as visitors walk among remnants of a civilization that thrived for centuries. The surrounding jungle adds to the allure, providing a tranquil atmosphere perfect for reflection and exploration.

Historical and Cultural Significance
Lamanai holds immense historical and cultural significance as one of the largest and most important Maya cities in Belize. The site has evidence of continuous occupation from 1500 B.C. to the Spanish conquest in the 17th century, highlighting its resilience and adaptability. Archaeological findings, including pottery and artifacts, provide insight into the daily lives of the Maya, their rituals, and their socio-political structures. Visiting Lamanai not only enriches one's understanding of Maya history but also emphasizes the importance of preserving such sites for future generations.

Activities and What to Do
There is much to do at Lamanai beyond simply exploring the ruins. Guided tours are available that provide in-depth information about the history and significance of each structure. Hiking trails wind through the jungle, offering opportunities to spot diverse wildlife, including howler monkeys, toucans, and iguanas. Visitors can also enjoy boat tours along the New River, where they might encounter crocodiles and a variety of bird species. The combination of archaeological exploration and immersive nature experiences makes Lamanai a well-rounded destination.

Photography Opportunities
For photography enthusiasts, Lamanai is a paradise filled with stunning visuals. The ancient temples, set against the backdrop of the dense jungle, create dramatic contrasts that are perfect for capturing the essence of Belize's natural

and historical beauty. Early morning light filters through the trees, illuminating the ruins in a magical way, while sunsets over the river provide breathtaking scenes. Every angle offers a new perspective, making it an ideal spot for anyone looking to document their travels.

Visitor Tips and Recommendations
Visitors are advised to wear comfortable walking shoes, as exploring the ruins involves some hiking over uneven terrain. It's also essential to bring plenty of water and sun protection, as the tropical sun can be intense. Guided tours often provide insights that enhance the experience, so consider joining one to fully appreciate the history and culture of the site. Lastly, take your time to soak in the ambiance and marvel at the ancient architecture, creating lasting memories in this hidden gem.

4.8 Placencia Peninsula

Located along the southern coast of Belize, the Placencia Peninsula is a captivating destination that offers an idyllic blend of stunning beaches, vibrant culture, and adventure. Known for its picturesque landscapes and laid-back atmosphere, this charming peninsula stretches about 16 miles, flanked by the Caribbean Sea on one side and lush mangroves on the other. With its welcoming locals and a plethora of activities, Placencia is a true hidden gem waiting to be discovered by travelers seeking a slice of paradise.

Getting There

Reaching Placencia is an adventure in itself, as it can be accessed by land, sea, or air. Visitors can take a scenic drive from Belize City, which takes approximately three to four hours along the Hummingbird Highway, renowned for its beautiful views. Alternatively, local airlines like Tropic Air and Maya Island Air offer quick flights to Placencia from Belize City, making the journey in about 30 minutes. For those who prefer the sea, water taxis from nearby islands and coastal towns also provide a delightful route to this tropical haven.

Entry Fees and Accessibility

There are no entry fees to access Placencia, allowing visitors to explore the area freely. The peninsula is easy to navigate, with the main village and beach areas accessible by foot or bicycle. The friendly local atmosphere encourages exploration, and various shops, restaurants, and attractions are conveniently located within walking distance.

Why It's Worth Visiting

Placencia is worth visiting for its breathtaking beaches and diverse marine ecosystems. The peninsula boasts some of the most stunning beaches in Belize, characterized by soft white sands and crystal-clear waters. Visitors can enjoy swimming, sunbathing, or simply relaxing with a book while taking in the tropical scenery. The friendly and welcoming vibe of the community, combined with the stunning natural beauty, makes Placencia an inviting destination for every traveler.

Historical and Cultural Significance

The history of Placencia is rich and intertwined with the various cultures that have inhabited the area. Originally settled by the Maya, the peninsula later saw the arrival of Garifuna and Creole communities, contributing to its cultural diversity. Today, Placencia celebrates its heritage through music, dance, and vibrant festivals, such as the annual Lobster Fest and the Placencia Independence Day celebrations. Exploring this cultural tapestry offers visitors a deeper understanding of Belize's history and the local way of life.

Activities and What to Do

Placencia is a hub for outdoor enthusiasts, offering a wide range of activities for all interests. Snorkeling and scuba diving in nearby reefs, such as the Laughing Bird Caye National Park, allow visitors to witness the vibrant marine life up close. Kayaking through the mangroves provides a unique perspective on the peninsula's natural beauty, while fishing trips cater to those seeking adventure on the open waters. For a more relaxed experience, visitors can stroll along the picturesque beachwalk or savor local cuisine at beachfront restaurants.

Culinary Delights and Local Cuisine
The culinary scene in Placencia is a highlight for many visitors, with numerous eateries serving fresh seafood and local specialties. From casual beach bars to upscale dining, the options are diverse and flavorful. Trying freshly caught lobster or conch, often prepared in traditional Belizean styles, is a must. The lively atmosphere of local restaurants, accompanied by ocean views, creates a memorable dining experience that embodies the essence of the peninsula.

Accommodations and Local Hospitality
Placencia offers a variety of accommodations to suit every budget and preference, ranging from cozy guesthouses to luxurious beachfront resorts. Many hotels and lodges reflect the local culture, providing warm hospitality and personalized service. Staying on the peninsula allows visitors to wake up to stunning sunrises and the sound of waves, enhancing the overall experience. The local community is known for its friendliness, ensuring that every traveler feels at home.

4.9 Hopkins Village
Located along the Caribbean coast of Belize, Hopkins Village is a vibrant coastal town that captivates visitors with its rich culture and stunning scenery. Located approximately 40 miles south of Belize City, this charming village is known for its pristine beaches, friendly locals, and the rhythmic sounds of Garifuna music. As a hidden gem, Hopkins offers a unique blend of relaxation and adventure, making it an ideal destination for travelers seeking an authentic Belizean experience.

Getting There
Reaching Hopkins Village is straightforward and scenic. Travelers can easily access the village by car or shuttle from Belize City, which takes about an hour and a half. Alternatively, visitors can take a bus from the city to nearby towns like Dangriga and then catch a short taxi ride to Hopkins. The journey through lush landscapes and coastal views sets the stage for the tranquil experience that awaits in this quaint village.

Entry Fees and Accessibility
Hopkins Village does not charge entry fees, making it an affordable destination for all travelers. The village is small and easily navigable on foot, allowing visitors to explore at their leisure. Many of the local attractions, including the beach and cultural sites, are accessible without any restrictions, fostering an inviting atmosphere. This accessibility encourages visitors to immerse themselves in the community and experience local life firsthand.

Why It's Worth Visiting
Hopkins Village is worth visiting for its captivating blend of natural beauty and cultural richness. The village boasts stunning beaches with soft white sand and clear blue waters, perfect for sunbathing or swimming. Additionally, the warm and welcoming locals create an inviting environment, making it easy for visitors to feel at home. Whether you're looking to relax or engage in activities, Hopkins offers something for everyone, ensuring an unforgettable getaway.

Historical and Cultural Significance
Hopkins is renowned for its strong Garifuna culture, which is reflected in the village's traditions, music, and cuisine. The Garifuna people, descendants of African, Arawak, and Carib ancestry, have a rich history that is celebrated through vibrant festivals and performances. Visitors can learn about this unique heritage at local cultural centers and through community events, deepening their understanding of Belize's diverse cultural landscape. The preservation of Garifuna traditions enriches the experience of every traveler.

Activities and What to Do
Hopkins Village offers a plethora of activities for visitors of all interests. Water sports enthusiasts can indulge in kayaking, paddleboarding, and snorkeling in the nearby barrier reef, where colorful marine life abounds. For those looking to explore inland, guided tours to the lush jungles, waterfalls, and ancient Mayan ruins provide a thrilling adventure. The village also hosts cultural events, such as drumming workshops, allowing visitors to engage with the local community and learn about Garifuna traditions firsthand.

Culinary Delights and Local Cuisine
The culinary scene in Hopkins is a delightful journey for the taste buds, featuring an array of local dishes that highlight the flavors of Garifuna culture. Seafood is a staple, with fresh catches served in various preparations, from

grilled fish to conch fritters. Local restaurants offer an inviting atmosphere where visitors can savor traditional dishes like hudut, a coconut-based fish stew served with plantains. Dining in Hopkins is more than just a meal; it's an opportunity to experience the vibrant culture through food.

Accommodations and Local Hospitality
Hopkins Village offers a range of accommodations, from cozy guesthouses to beachfront resorts, catering to different budgets and preferences. Many local establishments reflect the village's welcoming spirit, with hosts eager to share their culture and provide personalized recommendations. Staying in Hopkins allows visitors to embrace the slow pace of life and enjoy the tranquility of the Caribbean coast, making it an ideal retreat for relaxation.

4.10 Garifuna Settlements

The Garifuna Settlement is a vibrant cultural experience that showcases the rich heritage of the Garifuna people, a unique Afro-Indigenous group in Belize. Located primarily along the southern coast, particularly in towns like Dangriga and Punta Gorda, these settlements offer an immersive glimpse into the customs, music, and culinary delights of the Garifuna community. For visitors seeking authenticity and connection to local culture, exploring the Garifuna Settlement is an unforgettable journey.

Getting There
Reaching the Garifuna Settlement is straightforward, with various transportation options available. Visitors can fly into Belize City and then take a bus or shuttle to Dangriga, which is about a two-hour journey. From there, local taxis and water taxis can transport you to nearby Garifuna villages. The accessibility of these settlements makes it easy for travelers to explore this cultural gem without much hassle.

Entry Fees and Accessibility
There are generally no entry fees to the Garifuna settlements themselves, allowing for an open and welcoming experience. However, some cultural events, such as the annual Garifuna Settlement Day on November 19th, may have specific activities that require a small fee. The settlements are pedestrian-friendly, encouraging visitors to stroll through the streets, interact with locals, and engage in community activities. This accessibility enhances the authentic feel of the experience.

Why It's Worth Visiting
Visiting the Garifuna Settlement is worth it for the unique opportunity to experience a living culture that has preserved its traditions and customs for generations. The vibrant music, especially the lively rhythms of punta and paranda, invites visitors to join in the celebrations. The warm hospitality of the Garifuna people, combined with their rich cultural heritage, creates an inviting atmosphere that captivates the hearts of all who visit.

Historical and Cultural Significance
The Garifuna people have a fascinating history, stemming from the intermixing of West African, Carib, and Arawak ancestry. Recognized by UNESCO for their cultural significance, the Garifuna maintain a distinct identity through language, music, and dance. Their rich oral history and storytelling traditions reflect the struggles and resilience of their ancestors, making a visit to the settlements an enlightening experience that deepens one's appreciation for Belize's diverse heritage.

Activities and What to Do
Visitors to the Garifuna Settlement can immerse themselves in a variety of cultural activities. Participating in traditional drumming and dancing workshops allows guests to learn the vibrant rhythms that define Garifuna music. Culinary experiences, such as cooking classes featuring dishes like hudut (a fish and plantain stew), provide a delicious way to connect with the culture. Exploring local markets offers insight into traditional crafts and artisanal products, further enriching the experience.

Culinary Delights and Local Cuisine
Garifuna cuisine is a delightful fusion of flavors that reflects the community's rich heritage. Dishes often feature fresh seafood, coconut, and local vegetables, creating a unique culinary landscape. Popular offerings like cassava bread and ceviche highlight the island's abundance and the Garifuna's connection to the sea. Dining in a local eatery, surrounded by the sounds of music and laughter, makes for a memorable experience.

Accommodations and Local Hospitality
Accommodations in Garifuna settlements range from cozy guesthouses to beachfront lodges, allowing visitors to choose a stay that suits their preferences. Many establishments are family-run, providing a warm, homey atmosphere that

enhances the sense of community. The hospitality of the Garifuna people ensures that every guest feels welcome and can enjoy a personalized experience during their stay.

4.11 Outdoor Activities and Adventures

Snorkeling the Belize Barrier Reef
Snorkeling at the Belize Barrier Reef offers an unforgettable journey into a vibrant underwater paradise. As you glide through crystal-clear waters, colorful coral formations and schools of tropical fish surround you, creating an enchanting spectacle. Popular spots like Hol Chan Marine Reserve and Shark Ray Alley allow you to encounter friendly nurse sharks and majestic rays up close. The reef's diverse marine life, including sea turtles and vibrant coral gardens, captivates both novice and experienced snorkelers alike. This immersive experience invites you to explore one of the world's most biodiverse ecosystems, making it an essential adventure for every visitor.

Cave Tubing in the Caves of Belize
Cave tubing in Belize is an exhilarating way to experience the country's stunning natural beauty and rich history. As you float along the gentle currents of the Caves Branch River, you'll journey through ancient limestone caves adorned with impressive stalactites and stalagmites. The lush rainforest

surrounds you, providing a sense of serenity as you listen to the sounds of nature. Guided tours often share fascinating insights into the Mayan civilization, as these caves were once sacred sites for rituals. This unique adventure combines relaxation with exploration, offering a memorable connection to Belize's intriguing past.

Hiking in the Mountain Pine Ridge Forest Reserve
Hiking in the Mountain Pine Ridge Forest Reserve unveils Belize's breathtaking landscapes and rich biodiversity. As you traverse winding trails through towering pine trees and lush vegetation, the fresh mountain air invigorates your senses. The reserve is home to stunning waterfalls like Big Rock Falls, where you can take a refreshing dip after your hike. Wildlife enthusiasts will delight in spotting exotic birds and unique flora along the trails. This adventure invites you to immerse yourself in Belize's natural beauty, making it a perfect escape for nature lovers.

Zip Lining through the Canopy
Zip lining through the canopy of Belize's lush rainforests is an adrenaline-pumping adventure that offers a unique perspective on the vibrant ecosystem. Suspended high above the ground, you soar from tree to tree, experiencing the thrill of gliding through the treetops. Each zip line provides a breathtaking view of the sprawling jungle below, with the sounds of chirping birds and rustling leaves enveloping you. Many zip line tours include guided treks through the forest, educating visitors about the diverse wildlife and plant species. This exhilarating experience allows you to connect with nature while enjoying the thrill of flight.

Exploring the Ancient Ruins of Tikal
Exploring the ancient ruins of Tikal is a captivating journey into the heart of the Mayan civilization. Located just across the border in Guatemala, Tikal boasts impressive temples and pyramids that rise majestically above the jungle canopy. As you wander through the archaeological site, the sounds of howler monkeys and the rustle of wildlife surround you, bringing the ruins to life. Climbing the steep steps of Temple IV offers a stunning panoramic view of the surrounding rainforest, a sight that is both awe-inspiring and humbling. This adventure allows visitors to delve deep into the rich history of the Maya, creating a profound connection to the past.

4.12 Guided Tours and Recommended Tour Operators

Belize Adventure Tours

Belize Adventure Tours is renowned for its immersive experiences that blend adventure with cultural discovery. Offering a range of activities from snorkeling the Barrier Reef to exploring ancient Mayan ruins, their knowledgeable guides ensure a memorable journey. Visitors can easily book their tours online at (https://www.belizeadventuretours.com), making it convenient to plan an exciting itinerary.

Chaa Creek Eco-Lodge

Chaa Creek Eco-Lodge provides not only luxurious accommodations but also expertly guided tours through Belize's natural wonders. Guests can partake in hiking, birdwatching, and Mayan site tours, all led by experienced local guides. More information about their eco-friendly tours can be found on their website at (https://www.chaacreek.com), where visitors can customize their Belizean adventure.

Island Expeditions

Island Expeditions specializes in eco-adventures that showcase the beauty of Belize's islands and reefs. With a focus on kayaking, snorkeling, and cultural experiences, their tours cater to various interests and skill levels. For those eager to explore Belize's diverse landscapes, more details and bookings can be made at (https://www.islandexpeditions.com), ensuring an unforgettable adventure.

EcoTourism Belize

EcoTourism Belize emphasizes sustainable tourism while providing guided excursions into the country's lush rainforests and pristine waters. Their expert guides offer insightful commentary on the local flora, fauna, and the importance of conservation. Visitors can learn more and plan their eco-friendly excursions at (https://www.ecotourismbelize.com/), where unique experiences await.

Belize Luxury Tours

Belize Luxury Tours caters to travelers seeking high-end experiences combined with exceptional service. They offer tailored private tours that include everything from cultural excursions to adventure activities, ensuring a personalized journey. To discover their range of exclusive offerings, interested visitors can visit (https://www.belizeluxurytours.com), where they can begin crafting their dream vacation.

CHAPTER 5

PRACTICAL INFORMATION AND GUIDANCE

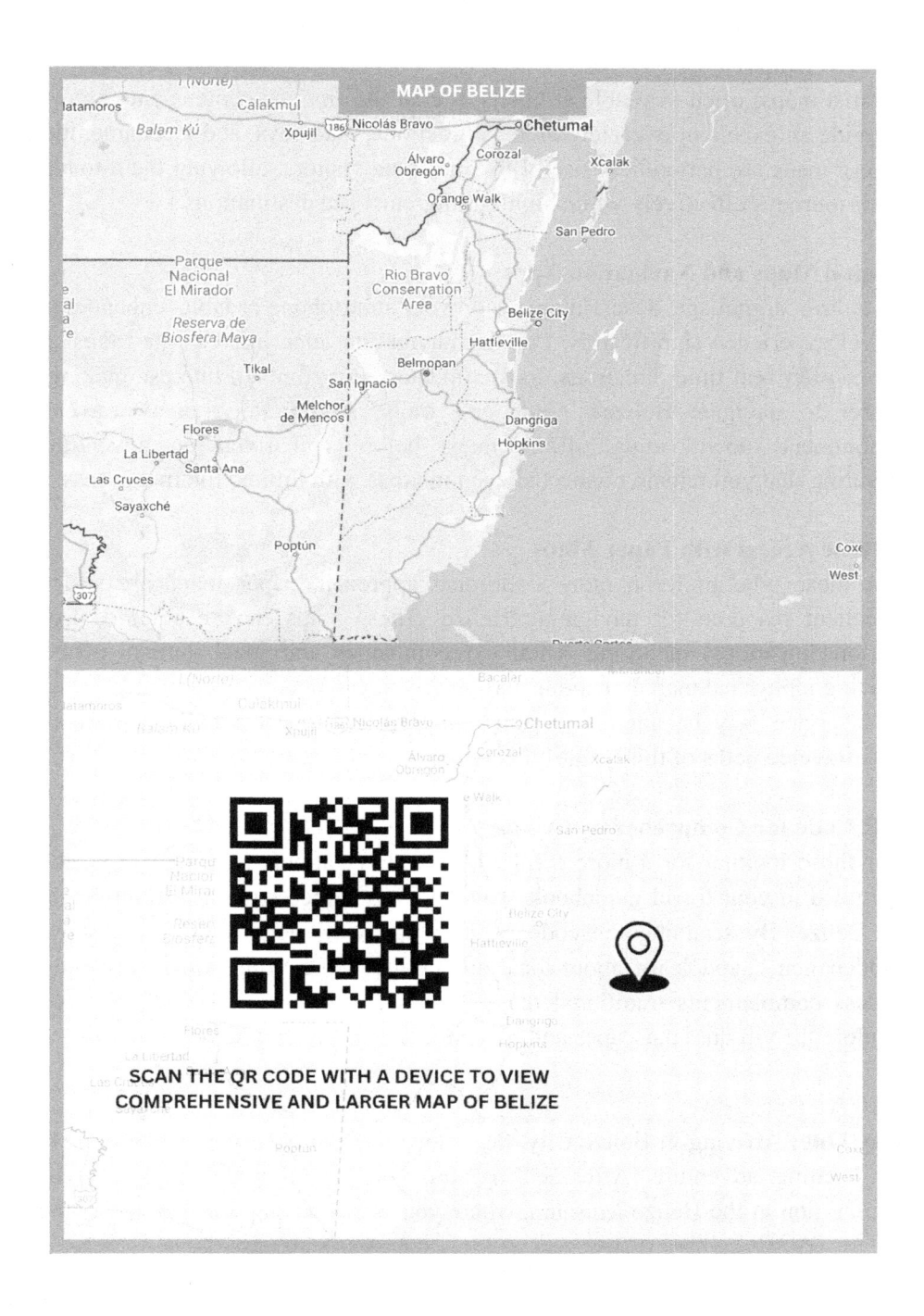

SCAN THE QR CODE WITH A DEVICE TO VIEW COMPREHENSIVE AND LARGER MAP OF BELIZE

5.1 Maps and Navigation

Navigating Belize can be an enriching experience, thanks to a variety of maps available to help visitors explore this beautiful country.

Tourist Maps

Tourist maps, often available at hotels, tourist information centers, and airports, provide an excellent overview of key attractions, roadways, and local amenities. These maps are particularly useful for first-time visitors, allowing them to plan their journeys effectively while highlighting must-see destinations.

Digital Maps and Navigation Apps

In today's digital age, accessing maps on your smartphone or tablet enhances the travel experience significantly. Popular navigation apps like Google Maps and Waze offer real-time directions, traffic updates, and points of interest, making it easier to navigate Belize's roads and trails. Additionally, many travelers recommend downloading offline maps before embarking on adventures, ensuring that you remain connected even in areas with limited internet access.

Offline Access with Paper Maps

For those who prefer a more traditional approach, paper maps are still an excellent resource for navigating Belize. These maps can be obtained from various locations, including rental car companies and local tourism offices. Having a physical map on hand is particularly advantageous in rural areas where cell service may be unreliable, allowing travelers to confidently explore the less-traveled paths of this beautiful country.

QR Code for Comprehensive Maps

For those looking for a more comprehensive navigational resource, a QR code included in your travel guidebook provides instant access to an interactive map of Belize. By scanning the code, visitors can view detailed routes, discover hidden gems, and learn about local attractions at their fingertips. This digital access complements traditional maps, creating a seamless experience as you explore the vibrant landscapes and rich culture of Belize.

5.2 Five Days Itinerary

Day One: Arriving in Belize City, the gateway to the country, sets the stage for an exciting adventure. After settling into your accommodation, begin your exploration at the Belize Museum, where you can delve into the nation's history and culture through fascinating exhibits. Stroll along the picturesque waterfront and visit the iconic Swing Bridge, which offers a glimpse into the city's colonial past. As the sun sets, indulge in a culinary experience at a local restaurant, savoring traditional Belizean dishes such as rice and beans with stewed chicken, perfectly capturing the essence of the local cuisine.

Day Two: On your second day, embark on an unforgettable journey to the Belize Barrier Reef, a UNESCO World Heritage site and the second-largest reef system in the world. Arrange a snorkeling or diving tour to explore the vibrant marine life, including colorful corals, tropical fish, and perhaps even sea turtles. Popular spots like Hol Chan Marine Reserve and Shark Ray Alley offer incredible underwater experiences. After a day of aquatic adventures, return to your lodging and unwind, reminiscing about the breathtaking sights and the vibrant underwater world you encountered.

Day Three: Day three takes you to the ancient Mayan ruins of Altun Ha, located just a short drive from Belize City. As you explore the well-preserved temples and plazas, you'll gain insight into the fascinating history of the Mayan civilization. Climb to the top of Temple of the Sun for stunning panoramic views of the surrounding jungle. After your exploration, enjoy a leisurely picnic lunch in the area, surrounded by lush vegetation. In the afternoon, return to Belize City and visit the nearby Belize Zoo, where you can encounter native wildlife in their natural habitats, enriching your understanding of the local ecosystem.

Day Four: Your fourth day leads you to the Cayo District, known for its breathtaking landscapes and outdoor adventures. Start your day with a visit to the Mountain Pine Ridge Forest Reserve, where you can hike to the stunning Big Rock Falls. The serene environment and refreshing waters make it an ideal spot for a picnic. In the afternoon, consider going cave tubing in the nearby Caves Branch River, floating through impressive limestone caves adorned with stunning formations. This adventure combines relaxation with exploration, offering a unique perspective on Belize's natural beauty.

Day Five: On your final day, take a short boat ride to the idyllic island of Caye Caulker, a perfect place to unwind and soak in the Caribbean atmosphere. Spend the day lounging on the sandy beaches or snorkeling in the warm, clear waters. The island's laid-back vibe allows you to relax and enjoy fresh seafood at local eateries. Before your departure, don't forget to visit the famous "Split," where you can take a refreshing dip. As you prepare to leave, reflect on your unforgettable five-day journey through Belize, filled with adventure, culture, and natural beauty that will linger in your memories long after you return home.

5.3 Essential Packing List

Clothing for Tropical Comfort

When packing for Belize, lightweight and breathable clothing is essential to cope with the tropical climate. Choose loose-fitting shirts, shorts, and sundresses made from natural fabrics to ensure comfort in the heat. Don't forget a light rain jacket, as tropical showers can occur unexpectedly, especially during the rainy season. Additionally, consider bringing a swimsuit for beach outings and water activities, ensuring you're always ready for adventure.

Footwear for Every Occasion

The right footwear is crucial for navigating both urban and natural environments in Belize. Comfortable sandals or flip-flops are ideal for beach days and casual outings, while sturdy hiking shoes or sneakers are necessary for exploring ruins and national parks. Water shoes can also be beneficial for snorkeling and kayaking, providing protection and traction in aquatic environments. Remember, good footwear enhances your overall experience, allowing you to explore freely and comfortably.

Essential Travel Documents

Having your travel documents in order is vital for a smooth journey to Belize. Ensure your passport is valid for at least six months beyond your arrival date, and check if you need a visa depending on your nationality. It's wise to carry printed copies of your itinerary, accommodation details, and any travel insurance documents. Additionally, keep a digital backup of important documents on your phone or cloud storage for easy access in case of emergencies.

Health and Safety Items

Packing health and safety essentials will help you stay protected during your travels. Bring a basic first aid kit containing band-aids, antiseptic wipes, and any personal medications you may need. Insect repellent is crucial for warding off mosquitoes, especially in jungle areas, while sunscreen will protect your skin from the sun's rays. A reusable water bottle is also recommended, as staying hydrated is vital in Belize's warm climate, and many places offer refills.

Tech Gear and Navigation Aids
Having the right tech gear enhances your travel experience in Belize. A smartphone with a good camera is perfect for capturing the stunning scenery and wildlife. Consider downloading offline maps and navigation apps before your trip, as they can assist you in exploring remote areas. A portable charger or power bank will ensure your devices remain charged throughout the day, allowing you to stay connected and navigate effortlessly during your adventures.

Beach and Water Activity Essentials
If you plan to enjoy Belize's beautiful beaches and water activities, packing the right gear is essential. Bring a beach towel and a waterproof dry bag to keep your belongings safe during water excursions. Snorkeling gear can be rented, but if you have your own, it might be more comfortable and familiar. Don't forget a good book or a journal for those lazy beach days, allowing you to unwind while soaking in the sun.

5.4 Setting Your Travel Budget

Setting a travel budget for Belize requires careful consideration of various factors, as this beautiful Central American destination offers a range of experiences that can fit different financial plans. It's essential to consider accommodation, transportation, activities, and food when crafting your budget. With thoughtful planning, you can enjoy all that Belize has to offer without overspending, ensuring a fulfilling experience that doesn't strain your finances.

Accommodation Expenses
Accommodation choices in Belize vary widely, catering to different budgets and preferences. From luxury resorts to budget hostels, prices can range from $20 per night for a basic dormitory to upwards of $300 for high-end lodging. Mid-range hotels typically cost between $70 and $150 per night, providing comfortable amenities without breaking the bank. Remember to factor in additional costs for taxes and service fees that may apply to your stay.

Transportation Costs
Transportation within Belize can significantly impact your overall budget, so it's important to choose options that suit your travel style. Public buses are an

economical way to travel between cities, with fares typically ranging from $5 to $25 depending on the distance. For those seeking more comfort or convenience, renting a car or hiring a taxi may be preferable, but it comes with higher costs. Domestic flights are also available for longer distances, especially to the cayes, and can range from $100 to $200. Always consider travel time and convenience when deciding on your transportation method.

Activities and Excursions

Belize is rich in activities that cater to adventure seekers and cultural enthusiasts alike, and these experiences can vary in cost. Snorkeling tours on the Belize Barrier Reef, for example, generally range from $50 to $150 per person, depending on the duration and inclusions. Visiting ancient Mayan sites may require entrance fees of around $10 to $20, while guided tours can add to your expenses. It's beneficial to research and prioritize the activities that excite you most, allowing you to allocate your budget effectively and ensure a fulfilling itinerary.

Dining and Food Costs

Food in Belize reflects its diverse culture and is an integral part of the travel experience, with options to suit every budget. Street food and local eateries can provide delicious meals for as little as $5 to $15, offering an authentic taste of Belizean cuisine. Mid-range restaurants typically charge between $15 and $30 for a meal, while high-end dining establishments can reach $50 or more per person. To save costs, consider dining at local markets or preparing some meals if your accommodation allows for it. Exploring food options not only supports local businesses but also enhances your cultural experience.

5.5 Visa Requirements and Entry Procedures

When planning a visit to Belize, understanding visa requirements and entry procedures is essential to ensure a smooth arrival. Belize welcomes travelers from numerous countries, often allowing them to enter without a visa for short stays. However, knowing the specifics based on your nationality can prevent potential hassles at the border.

Visa Exemptions and Requirements

Citizens from many countries, including the United States, Canada, and most European nations, do not require a visa for stays of up to 30 days in Belize. For longer stays or for visitors from countries that do require a visa, it is essential to apply in advance at a Belizean consulate or embassy. Travelers should also have a valid passport, which must remain valid for at least six months beyond the intended departure date from Belize. Additionally, having proof of onward travel, such as a return ticket, can facilitate the entry process.

Immigration Procedures Upon Arrival
Upon arrival in Belize, travelers will go through immigration control, where officials will check passports and any necessary documentation. It's advisable to have your passport, completed customs declaration, and proof of onward travel ready for inspection. Visitors may also be asked about the purpose of their visit and their intended length of stay. The immigration process is typically straightforward, and travelers should expect to receive a visitor's stamp in their passport, which allows them to stay for the duration permitted.

Customs Regulations to Note
Belize has specific customs regulations that visitors should be aware of when entering the country. Travelers are allowed to bring in a reasonable amount of personal items, but certain restrictions apply to items such as food, agricultural products, and large amounts of cash. It's important to declare any items that exceed the permitted limits to avoid fines or confiscation. Additionally, visitors should familiarize themselves with the regulations regarding duty-free allowances for alcohol and tobacco, ensuring compliance with local laws.

Extension of Stay Procedures
If you wish to extend your stay beyond the initial entry period, Belize provides options for doing so. Visitors can apply for an extension at the Immigration Department in Belize City or other authorized offices. Extensions are generally granted for an additional 30 days, but it's important to apply before your initial stay expires to avoid overstaying, which can lead to fines or difficulties in future travel. Having documentation, such as proof of accommodation and financial means to support your extended stay, will assist in the approval process.

5.6 Safety Tips and Emergency Contacts

Traveling to Belize can be an exhilarating experience, filled with stunning landscapes and rich cultural encounters. However, like any travel destination, ensuring your safety is paramount. Visitors should be aware of their surroundings and take precautionary measures to minimize risks while exploring this beautiful country. By understanding safety tips and knowing emergency contacts, you can enhance your experience and travel with peace of mind, making the most of your time in Belize.

General Safety Tips for Travelers
When exploring Belize, it's important to stay vigilant, particularly in crowded areas or when using public transportation. Keep your belongings secure and avoid displaying valuable items, such as expensive jewelry or electronics, to deter theft. Stick to well-lit and populated areas, especially at night, and consider traveling with a group for added safety. Familiarizing yourself with local customs and cultural norms can also help you blend in and avoid inadvertently causing offense. Lastly, trust your instincts; if something feels off, it's best to remove yourself from the situation.

Health and Medical Precautions
Health safety is a critical aspect of traveling in Belize, where access to medical facilities may vary, especially in rural areas. Travelers should consider obtaining travel insurance that covers medical emergencies to ensure they receive adequate care if needed. It's advisable to bring a basic first-aid kit, including essential medications, insect repellent, and sunscreen, as well as to stay hydrated, particularly in the tropical climate. Be aware of any health advisories, such as mosquito-borne diseases, and take necessary precautions, including vaccinations if recommended. Understanding local health services can also be beneficial in case of illness or injury.

Emergency Contacts to Know
In case of an emergency, knowing whom to contact can make all the difference. The local emergency services number in Belize is 911, which can be used for police, fire, and medical assistance. Additionally, it's helpful to have the contact information for your country's embassy or consulate in Belize, as they can provide assistance in various situations, including lost passports or legal issues. Travelers should also consider keeping a list of local hospitals and clinics, especially if venturing into more remote areas. Familiarizing yourself with these resources can empower you to act swiftly in emergencies.

Personal Safety Measures
Practicing personal safety measures can significantly enhance your security while traveling. Always inform someone about your plans and share your itinerary, especially if you are traveling alone or to less frequented areas.

Utilizing reputable tour operators for excursions can provide not only convenience but also a layer of safety, as these companies are familiar with local conditions. Avoid excessive alcohol consumption that may impair your judgment, and keep your accommodation's contact information easily accessible. By being proactive and aware, you can mitigate risks and enjoy your journey with confidence.

5.7 Currency Exchange and Banking Services

When traveling to Belize, understanding the currency exchange and banking services is crucial for a seamless experience. The official currency is the Belize dollar (BZD), which is subdivided into 100 cents. While the Belize dollar is widely accepted, many establishments, particularly in tourist areas, also accept the US dollar (USD) at a fixed exchange rate, making transactions convenient for visitors. Familiarizing yourself with the local currency and banking options will ensure that you can manage your finances effectively during your stay in this beautiful Central American country.

Currency Exchange Options

Currency exchange in Belize can be easily accessed at banks, hotels, and dedicated currency exchange offices. Most major banks offer currency exchange services, providing competitive rates and a secure environment for transactions. Visitors should note that while US dollars are accepted, receiving change in Belize dollars is common, so being prepared to handle both currencies is advisable. ATMs are also widely available in urban areas, allowing travelers to withdraw cash in Belize dollars. However, it's essential to check with your bank regarding international withdrawal fees before using these services.

Banking Services and Hours

Banking services in Belize are generally reliable and cater to both locals and tourists. Major banks such as Belize Bank, Atlantic Bank, and Scotiabank have branches across the country, particularly in larger towns and cities. Banking hours typically run from Monday to Friday, with some banks open on Saturdays, but it's best to confirm specific hours as they can vary. Most banks offer a range of services, including checking accounts, savings accounts, and foreign currency exchange. Visitors may also find that some banks provide online banking options, allowing for easier account management during their travels.

Credit and Debit Card Usage

Credit and debit cards are accepted at many businesses in Belize, particularly in tourist hotspots, hotels, and restaurants. Visa and MasterCard are the most widely accepted, while American Express may not be as universally recognized. However, it's wise to carry cash for smaller purchases, as some vendors, especially in remote areas, may not accept cards. Additionally, travelers should notify their bank about their travel plans to avoid any issues with card usage due to fraud alerts. Keeping an eye on exchange rates and transaction fees associated with card use can also help in managing expenses effectively.

Safety Considerations for Financial Transactions

While Belize is generally safe for tourists, it's important to take precautions when handling currency and banking transactions. Avoid carrying large amounts of cash and instead use secure methods to store your money, such as a hotel safe. When using ATMs, opt for those located in well-lit, populated areas, preferably within bank branches. Always cover the keypad while entering your PIN and be cautious of your surroundings to prevent theft or fraud. By following these safety tips, visitors can protect themselves while enjoying the convenience of financial services in Belize.

5.8 Language, Communication and Useful Phrases

Belize is a melting pot of cultures, and its linguistic diversity reflects this rich heritage. English is the official language, making communication relatively easy for English-speaking visitors. However, the country's multilingualism adds to the charm of the travel experience, with Spanish, Kriol, Garifuna, and Maya dialects also widely spoken. Understanding the local languages and useful phrases not only enhances your interactions with locals but also offers a deeper connection to Belize's unique cultural blend.

English as the Official Language

As the only English-speaking country in Central America, Belize provides an accessible and welcoming environment for English-speaking travelers. English is used in official settings, such as government offices, schools, and businesses. For tourists, this means that finding your way around, asking for directions, and reading signs or menus is straightforward. Even though English is the official language, learning some local phrases can enrich your experience and show respect for the diverse cultures that call Belize home.

The Influence of Kriol
Belizean Kriol, a creole language rooted in English, is commonly spoken across the country. While Kriol is similar to English, it has its own distinct grammar and expressions. Many Belizeans speak Kriol in informal settings, and it acts as a unifying language among the different ethnic groups. Visitors who take the time to pick up a few Kriol phrases will often find themselves greeted with smiles and appreciation. Phrases like "Weh di go aan?" (What's going on?) or "Mi deh yah" (I'm here) can be handy during casual conversations with locals.

Spanish and its Importance
Spanish is the second most spoken language in Belize, particularly in the northern and western regions near the border with Mexico and Guatemala. While English is the official language, many Belizeans are bilingual and fluent in Spanish. This is especially beneficial for travelers from Spanish-speaking countries or those familiar with the language. In regions like Corozal and San Ignacio, using basic Spanish phrases such as "Hola" (Hello) and "Gracias" (Thank you) can help bridge communication gaps and foster a sense of connection with the local communities.

Garifuna and Maya Languages
The indigenous Garifuna and Maya communities in Belize preserve their unique languages and cultural traditions. In southern towns like Dangriga and Hopkins, Garifuna is widely spoken, and understanding a few words of this language can enhance your cultural experience. Similarly, Maya dialects like Mopan and Q'eqchi' are spoken in villages in the Toledo District. While English will serve you well, learning about these languages and their significance to the indigenous people adds depth to your travels, offering a glimpse into their enduring heritage.

Useful Phrases for Visitors
Knowing some useful phrases can go a long way in navigating Belize and building rapport with locals. Simple greetings and expressions, whether in English, Kriol, or Spanish, show a willingness to engage with the culture. A phrase like "Good maanin" (Good morning) or "How yu di du?" (How are you?) in Kriol can break the ice in everyday interactions. Politeness is highly valued in Belize, and saying "tank yu" (thank you) or "please" is always appreciated. The local dialects provide a cultural richness that elevates the travel experience, making each encounter more meaningful.

5.9 Shopping in Belize

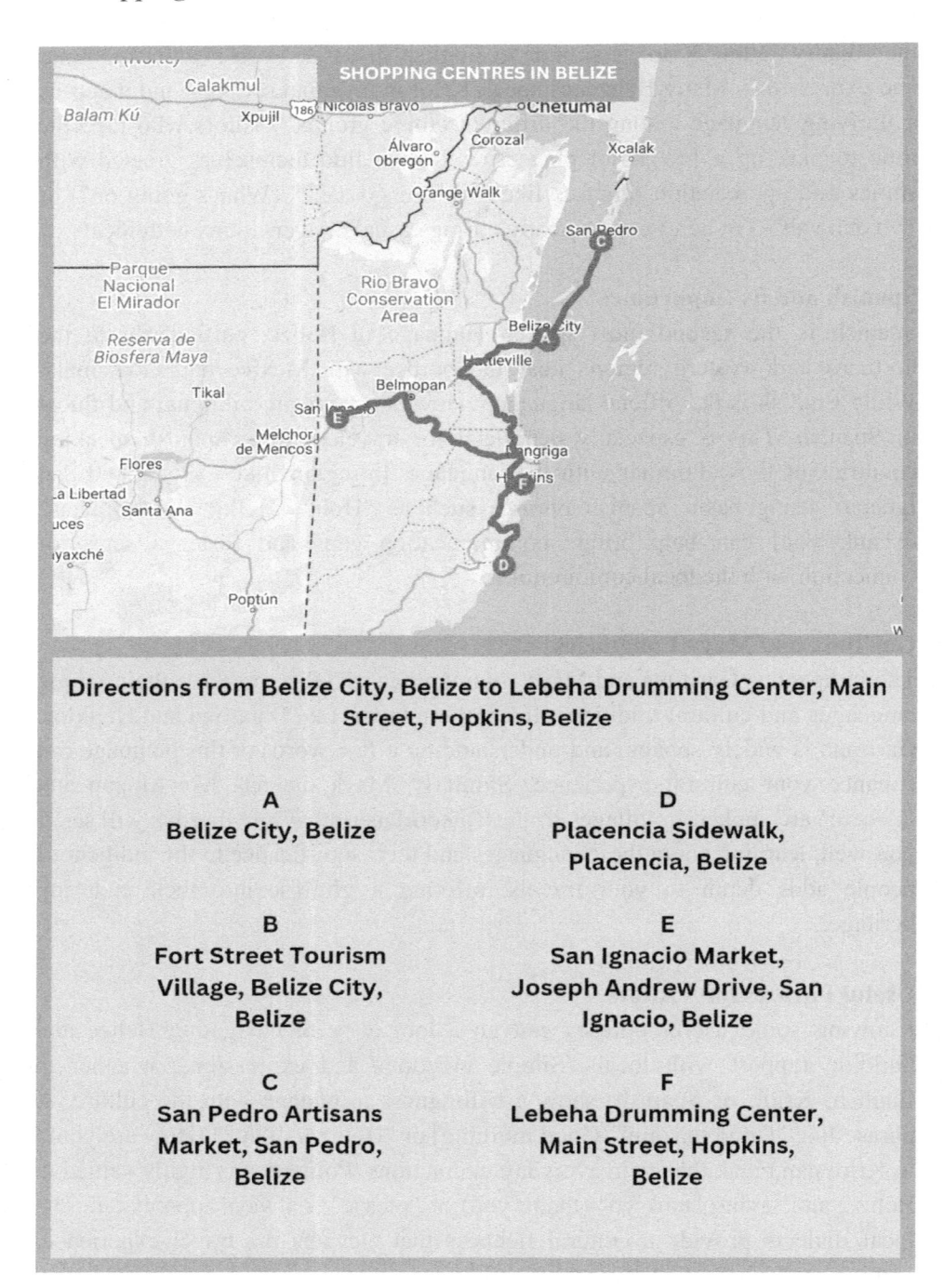

SHOPPING CENTRES IN BELIZE

Directions from Belize City, Belize to Lebeha Drumming Center, Main Street, Hopkins, Belize

A Belize City, Belize	**D** Placencia Sidewalk, Placencia, Belize
B Fort Street Tourism Village, Belize City, Belize	**E** San Ignacio Market, Joseph Andrew Drive, San Ignacio, Belize
C San Pedro Artisans Market, San Pedro, Belize	**F** Lebeha Drumming Center, Main Street, Hopkins, Belize

Belize offers a unique shopping experience, where visitors can find an array of locally crafted goods and authentic souvenirs. From bustling markets to boutique shops, the country is a treasure trove of handcrafted items, jewelry, and indigenous art. Whether you're in search of artisanal products or cultural memorabilia, the shopping destinations across Belize reflect the diverse heritage and creativity of its people.

Fort Street Tourism Village
Located in the heart of Belize City, Fort Street Tourism Village is a popular shopping hub for tourists. This waterfront shopping area is easily accessible from the cruise port and offers a variety of handcrafted jewelry, textiles, and Belizean souvenirs. You'll find everything from carved wooden items to Belizean rum and spices. The village is designed to cater to visitors, making it convenient for anyone looking for a hassle-free shopping experience. Its vibrant atmosphere and array of shops provide plenty of options to pick up mementos that represent Belizean culture.

Artisan's Market, San Pedro
In the coastal town of San Pedro on Ambergris Caye, the Artisan's Market is a must-visit for those seeking authentic local crafts. Located near the town center, it's easily accessible by foot or golf cart, which are popular modes of transport on the island. The market specializes in handmade items such as intricate woven baskets, vibrant paintings, and traditional Garifuna drums. It's a fantastic place to purchase unique Belizean crafts directly from the artisans, offering insight into the techniques and traditions behind each piece.

Placencia sidewalk
Placencia's famous sidewalk is home to a collection of small arts and gift shops that line the narrow pedestrian path. Here, visitors can find a variety of locally produced goods including organic skincare products, hand-painted ceramics, and tropical-themed clothing. The charm of this shopping area lies in its relaxed, beach-town atmosphere, and the friendly interactions with local shop owners. Accessible by car or bike, Placencia offers a serene and enjoyable shopping experience while you browse for one-of-a-kind Belizean souvenirs.

San Ignacio Market
San Ignacio, located in the Cayo District, boasts a vibrant open-air market that draws both locals and tourists alike. The market is known for its fresh produce,

but it also features vendors selling Belizean crafts, clothing, and herbal remedies. Held every Saturday, the market becomes a lively spot where you can engage with local vendors and learn about the traditions behind their goods. Easily accessible by foot from most accommodations in the town, San Ignacio Market is a perfect stop for those interested in authentic local shopping.

National Handicraft Center, Belmopan
Belmopan's National Handicraft Center, located near the city center, is dedicated to showcasing and selling Belizean artisanal products. The center features a range of handcrafted items, including pottery, textiles, and jewelry, all made by local artisans. It's a government-supported initiative aimed at preserving and promoting Belize's rich cultural heritage. The center is easily accessible by bus or car and offers an authentic shopping experience where visitors can purchase souvenirs that reflect the heart of Belize's craftsmanship.

Lebeha Drumming Center Gift Shop, Hopkins
Hopkins, a village rich in Garifuna culture, offers a unique shopping experience at the Lebeha Drumming Center Gift Shop. Located near the beach, this small store specializes in Garifuna-inspired crafts, including handmade drums, vibrant textiles, and musical instruments. Visitors can purchase items that reflect the vibrant cultural traditions of the Garifuna people while supporting local artisans. The shop is an excellent stop for those looking to bring home an authentic piece of Belizean culture, all while enjoying the sounds of live drumming performances nearby.

5.10 Health and Wellness Centers

Serenity Spa and Wellness Center
Serenity Spa and Wellness Center is located in San Pedro on Ambergris Caye, offering a peaceful escape for travelers seeking relaxation. The center provides a variety of treatments, including massages, facials, and body wraps using organic products. Their beachfront location enhances the calming experience, allowing visitors to unwind to the sounds of the ocean. The spa offers a range of packages designed for ultimate rejuvenation after a long day of exploring Belize's wonders.

Naïa Resort and Spa
Situated in Placencia, Naïa Resort and Spa is located within a lush, natural landscape that complements its wellness offerings. The spa is renowned for its

immersive experience, with open-air treatment rooms that overlook the serene lagoon. Services range from traditional massages to specialized treatments that incorporate Belizean ingredients. You can reach Naïa at +501-523-4600 for appointments and wellness packages. This is a haven for those looking to reconnect with nature while indulging in holistic health treatments.

Belize Yoga Retreat
Located in the tranquil village of Hopkins, Belize Yoga Retreat offers both yoga and wellness services for those seeking a more spiritual journey. The retreat specializes in yoga classes, meditation sessions, and holistic therapies such as sound healing. Visitors are encouraged to immerse themselves in the calming environment, with easy access to the beach and local nature trails. For more information, contact them via email at info@belizeyogaretreat.com. This center provides a perfect escape for mental and physical rejuvenation.

The Spa at Las Terrazas
The Spa at Las Terrazas, located on Ambergris Caye, is known for its luxurious services tailored to travelers seeking relaxation in a tropical setting. Their treatments include hot stone massages, deep tissue therapies, and anti-aging facials, using eco-friendly products. The spa is part of Las Terrazas Resort, a popular destination for wellness seekers. You can contact them at +501-226-4249 to schedule a treatment. With its oceanfront location, the spa offers a perfect blend of luxury and natural beauty.

Ahki Retreat Belize
Ahki Retreat Belize is located in the northern district of Corozal, surrounded by lush gardens and the tranquility of the countryside. Specializing in holistic wellness, the retreat offers detox programs, yoga classes, and spa treatments that focus on healing and relaxation. The serene environment allows visitors to disconnect from daily stresses and engage in self-care. Contact them at +501-623-3487 to learn more about their programs and availability. It's the ideal retreat for those looking to focus on their health in a peaceful, natural setting.

5.11 Useful Websites, Mobile Apps and Online Resources

Belize Tourism Board Website
The official website of the Belize Tourism Board, found at www.travelbelize.org, is an essential resource for travelers planning their visit to Belize. The site offers comprehensive information on attractions,

accommodations, and activities across the country. Visitors can find travel tips, important updates, and curated itineraries that make planning effortless.

TripAdvisor Belize
TripAdvisor's Belize section, accessible at www.tripadvisor.com/Belize, is a reliable platform for finding reviews, recommendations, and travel tips from previous visitors. The site covers everything from the best local restaurants to hidden gems in Belize. It also offers booking options for hotels, tours, and activities, giving visitors a complete planning experience.

Belize Bus Schedule App
The Belize Bus Schedule mobile app is an indispensable tool for navigating the local bus system. Available for both Android and iOS, the app provides real-time information on bus routes, schedules, and fares across Belize. It is particularly useful for budget travelers relying on public transportation to explore the country efficiently.

Google Maps
Google Maps, accessible at www.google.com/maps, is an invaluable tool for navigating Belize's cities, towns, and rural areas. It provides detailed directions, points of interest, and real-time traffic updates, making it easier for visitors to explore without getting lost. The offline mode is especially helpful for those in remote areas with limited internet access.

Airbnb Belize
Airbnb's platform, available at https://www.airbnb.com/belize/stays, offers an array of lodging options for travelers seeking authentic, local experiences. Visitors can find everything from beachfront cottages to jungle retreats, complete with reviews and detailed descriptions. The site also allows for seamless booking and direct communication with hosts for a personalized experience.

Belize Travel Guide App
The Belize Travel Guide mobile app is a comprehensive resource that offers in-depth information on attractions, local customs, and must-see sites. It includes features such as GPS-enabled maps, historical details, and restaurant suggestions. This app is ideal for independent travelers looking for quick, detailed insights during their trip.

5.12 Internet Access and Connectivity

As you embark on your journey to Belize, understanding the landscape of internet access and connectivity is essential. The country, renowned for its lush jungles and stunning coastline, offers a unique blend of modern conveniences amid its natural beauty. Major urban areas, such as Belize City and San Pedro, are equipped with relatively reliable internet services, allowing you to stay connected during your travels. However, it's important to note that internet speeds may vary, and rural areas can experience interruptions due to infrastructure challenges.

Mobile connectivity is prevalent, with several local providers offering data plans that can be conveniently purchased upon arrival. Visitors can acquire a prepaid SIM card at the airport or local shops, providing an immediate solution for staying in touch with family and friends back home. Coverage tends to be better in populated areas, while remote locations may lack signal, making it wise to plan ahead for excursions into the wilderness. Public Wi-Fi is available in many hotels, cafes, and restaurants, creating opportunities to connect while you enjoy local cuisine or sip on a refreshing beverage. However, the quality of these connections can vary, with some places offering robust signals while others may have sporadic service. As you explore the captivating landscapes, be prepared for moments of disconnection, which can serve as a perfect excuse to immerse yourself in the natural surroundings.

For those seeking a more stable connection, many hotels and resorts offer upgraded internet options for a fee. This can be a worthwhile investment if you require reliable access for work or streaming services. It's advisable to inquire about connectivity options upon booking your accommodation to ensure you have the desired level of access during your stay in this tropical paradise. Ultimately, while Belize may not boast the fastest internet speeds, the charm of the country lies in its unhurried pace and breathtaking vistas. Embrace the opportunity to disconnect from the digital world and reconnect with the beauty of nature and local culture. The moments spent exploring ancient ruins, diving into the turquoise waters, and engaging with friendly locals will undoubtedly create lasting memories far beyond what any online connection can offer.

5.13 Visitor Centers and Tourist Assistance

Belize Tourism Board Visitor Center
Located in Belize City, the Belize Tourism Board Visitor Center serves as a hub for travelers seeking information about attractions, accommodations, and tours. Visitors can access brochures, maps, and expert advice to enhance their trip. For more details, visit their website at www.travelbelize.org.

San Pedro Visitor Center
Situated on the picturesque Ambergris Caye, the San Pedro Visitor Center provides essential information on local activities, dining, and transportation options. Friendly staff are available to help plan your adventures and connect you with local guides. For assistance, contact them at sanpedro@travelbelize.org.

Cayo District Visitor Center
Located in San Ignacio, the Cayo District Visitor Center offers a wealth of resources for those exploring the lush jungles and Mayan ruins. Here, travelers can find maps, cultural insights, and recommendations for eco-tours and outdoor activities.

Placencia Tourist Information Center
Located in the vibrant village of Placencia, this center caters to visitors interested in the local culture, marine activities, and nearby attractions. Staffed by knowledgeable locals, they provide insights on everything from dining to guided tours. Reach out for more info via their website at https://www.placencia.com/..

CHAPTER 6
GASTRONOMIC DELIGHTS

6.1 Dining Options and Top Restaurants

Belize is a vibrant country known for its rich culture, stunning landscapes, and, of course, its delectable cuisine. The culinary scene here is a delightful blend of Caribbean flavors, traditional Maya ingredients, and influences from neighboring regions. From seaside shacks to elegant dining establishments, the dining options are as diverse as the country itself. Here, we explore six exceptional restaurants and cafés that reflect the unique flavors and ambiance of Belize.

Old River Bar & Grill

Located along the banks of the Belize River, The Old River Bar & Grill offers a rustic yet inviting atmosphere that perfectly complements its menu. This family-owned establishment prides itself on serving authentic Belizean dishes made from locally sourced ingredients. Guests can indulge in traditional staples such as stewed chicken, rice and beans, and freshly caught fish, all paired with house-made sauces and salsas that elevate the flavors. The bar is also known for its refreshing beverages, including fresh fruit juices and local Belizean beers.

The Old River Bar & Grill opens its doors daily from 11 AM to 10 PM, making it a perfect spot for both lunch and dinner. Its scenic riverside location provides a tranquil backdrop for a leisurely meal, and the friendly staff ensures that every visit feels like coming home. Whether you're a local or a visitor, this charming eatery offers an authentic taste of Belizean hospitality.

Café Nola
Located in the heart of San Ignacio, Café Nola is a delightful café that seamlessly combines Belizean flavors with international influences. The café's eclectic menu features an array of options, from hearty breakfast burritos to gourmet sandwiches and fresh salads. For those with a sweet tooth, the dessert selection is not to be missed, featuring homemade pastries and cakes that are perfect for a mid-afternoon treat. Café Nola operates from 7 AM to 6 PM, making it an ideal breakfast and lunch destination. The vibrant décor and warm atmosphere invite guests to linger, whether they're sipping a locally sourced coffee or enjoying a leisurely meal with friends. With its commitment to quality and creativity, Café Nola has become a beloved gathering spot for locals and travelers alike.

The Belize Chocolate Company
For chocolate lovers, The Belize Chocolate Company is a must-visit destination. Located in the coastal town of San Pedro, this artisanal chocolate shop offers a unique experience where visitors can learn about the chocolate-making process while indulging in exquisite treats. The shop specializes in bean-to-bar chocolate, ensuring that every piece reflects the rich, robust flavors of Belizean cacao. Guests can explore a variety of chocolate offerings, from dark chocolate bars infused with local spices to decadent truffles. The Belize Chocolate Company is open from 10 AM to 5 PM, and its warm, welcoming atmosphere makes it a delightful stop for anyone looking to satisfy their sweet cravings. Pair your chocolate experience with a refreshing smoothie or a cup of rich hot chocolate for the ultimate indulgence.

Elvi's Kitchen
Elvi's Kitchen, located in the bustling town of San Pedro, is renowned for its extensive menu that showcases the best of Belizean cuisine. With a history spanning over three decades, this family-run restaurant has become a staple for both locals and tourists. The menu features a wide range of dishes, including succulent lobster, grilled fish, and traditional Belizean fare like ceviche and

tamales. The ambiance at Elvi's Kitchen is casual yet inviting, with colorful decor and friendly service that enhances the dining experience. Open daily from 11 AM to 10 PM, this eatery is the perfect place for a leisurely lunch or a romantic dinner by the beach. The restaurant's commitment to using fresh, locally sourced ingredients ensures that every dish bursts with flavor, making it a culinary gem in Belize.

The Riverside Tavern
The Riverside Tavern, situated in the vibrant town of Belize City, is a popular spot for those looking to enjoy a lively atmosphere paired with delicious food and drinks. Known for its extensive drink menu, including a variety of local beers, cocktails, and specialty drinks, the tavern is a great place to unwind after a day of exploring. The food menu features a selection of pub-style fare, including burgers, wings, and seafood platters, all crafted with a Belizean twist. Open from 11 AM until midnight, the Riverside Tavern is perfect for both lunch and late-night gatherings. The casual, friendly vibe makes it a favorite among locals and visitors, ensuring that everyone leaves with a smile and a satisfied palate.

The Green Parrot
Perched along the beautiful shores of Ambergris Caye, The Green Parrot offers a delightful escape with breathtaking ocean views. This laid-back restaurant specializes in seafood, with a menu that highlights the freshest catches from the Caribbean Sea. Diners can enjoy dishes such as grilled snapper, shrimp tacos, and coconut curry, all accompanied by a selection of tropical cocktails and refreshing smoothies. The Green Parrot is open from 10 AM to 10 PM, making it an excellent choice for both lunch and dinner. The relaxed atmosphere, complete with hammocks and ocean breezes, invites guests to linger and soak in the stunning surroundings. With its commitment to providing a memorable dining experience, The Green Parrot remains a beloved destination for those seeking a taste of Belize's coastal charm.

RESTAURANTS IN BELIZE

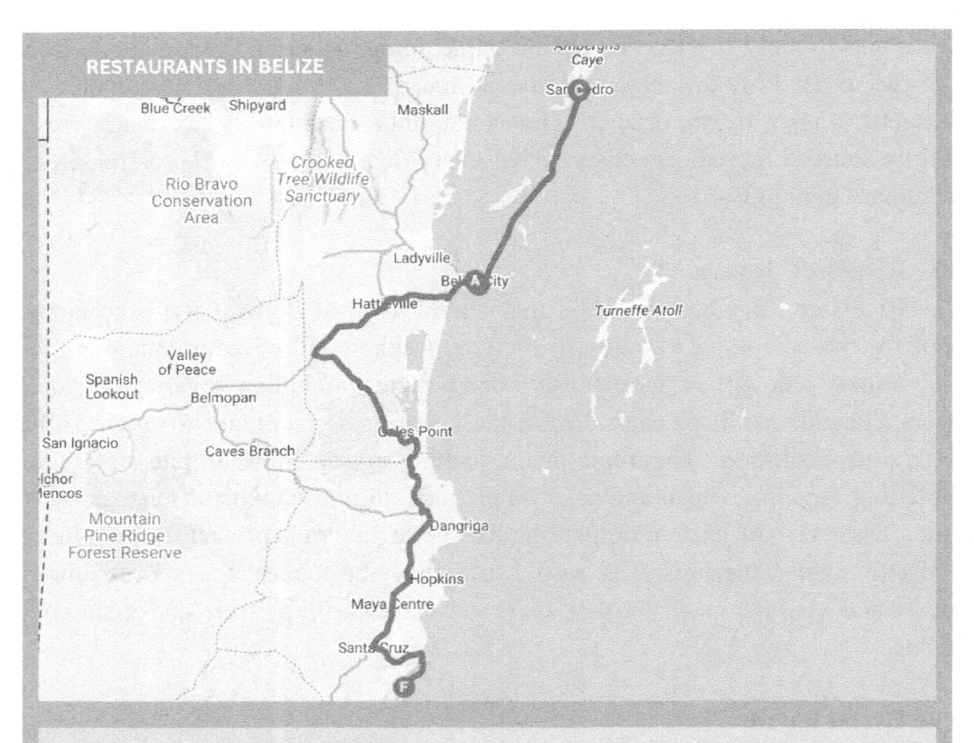

Directions from Old River Bar & Grill, Regent Street, Belize City, Belize to Belize City, Belize

A
Belize City, Belize

B
Old River Bar & Grill, Regent Street, Belize City, Belize

C
Belize Chocolate Company, San Pedro, Belize

D
Elvi's Kitchen, Pescador Drive San Pedro, Belize

E
Riverside Tavern, Mapp Street, Belize City, Belize

F
Green Parrot Resort-Pelican Pub & Grill, Placencia, Belize

6.2 Traditional Belizean Cuisine

Belize is a culinary treasure trove, reflecting its rich cultural heritage through an array of traditional dishes. The country's diverse population, composed of Maya, Creole, Garifuna, and Mestizo communities, has influenced its cuisine, resulting in a vibrant tapestry of flavors and ingredients. From hearty stews to fresh seafood, traditional Belizean cuisine offers a delightful experience for visitors. This exploration of six beloved dishes provides insight into where to find them, their prices, and valuable tips for an authentic culinary adventure in Belize.

Rice and Beans

One of the quintessential dishes of Belize is rice and beans, often served as a side or main course. This dish features fluffy white rice cooked with red kidney beans and flavored with coconut milk, spices, and herbs, creating a comforting and flavorful meal. Visitors can find rice and beans in many local eateries, from street vendors to family-run restaurants. Prices typically range from $5 to $10 USD, depending on the portion size and accompaniments. For an authentic experience, pair it with stewed chicken or grilled fish, and don't hesitate to ask for extra hot sauce to enhance the flavors.

Tamales

Tamales are a beloved traditional dish in Belize, made from masa (corn dough) filled with seasoned meat, vegetables, or even fruits, wrapped in banana leaves and steamed to perfection. These flavorful bundles are often enjoyed during special occasions but can also be found at local markets and roadside stalls. Prices for tamales generally range from $2 to $4 USD each. Visitors should look for vendors selling them fresh, as the best tamales are those made with care and served hot. Sampling tamales with a side of salsa or a drizzle of lime adds an extra layer of flavor to this delightful dish.

Fry Jacks

Fry jacks are a popular breakfast item in Belize, characterized by their fluffy, deep-fried dough that is typically served alongside eggs, beans, and fresh fruit. These golden delights can be found at most local breakfast spots, with prices ranging from $3 to $8 USD, depending on the portion and accompanying dishes. Visitors are encouraged to enjoy fry jacks with Belizean hot sauce for an authentic kick. The best fry jacks are light and airy, so seeking out a well-reviewed local café or diner will ensure a delicious start to the day.

Conch Fritters
Conch fritters are a must-try for seafood lovers visiting Belize, particularly in coastal towns like San Pedro. These tasty bites are made from minced conch meat mixed with spices, herbs, and batter, then deep-fried until golden brown. Served with a tangy dipping sauce, conch fritters offer a delightful blend of textures and flavors. Prices typically range from $10 to $15 USD for a plate. Visitors should seek out beachfront restaurants or local food stalls known for their fresh seafood, ensuring a delicious and authentic experience. Enjoying conch fritters with a cold local beer enhances this tropical culinary adventure.

Belizean Ceviche
Belizean ceviche is a refreshing dish made with fresh fish or shrimp marinated in lime juice, mixed with diced tomatoes, onions, cilantro, and peppers. This vibrant dish is popular among locals and tourists alike, especially on hot days. Ceviche can be found in various restaurants along the coast, with prices ranging from $8 to $15 USD, depending on the seafood used. Visitors are encouraged to try ceviche from places that emphasize fresh, local ingredients, ensuring the best flavor. Pairing ceviche with corn tortillas or tortilla chips adds a delightful crunch to this zesty dish.

Escabeche
Escabeche is a traditional Belizean soup that features chicken or fish cooked in a tangy vinegar-based broth, infused with onions, garlic, and spices. This dish is not only comforting but also boasts a unique balance of flavors that reflects Belize's culinary influences. Escabeche is commonly served in local restaurants, with prices ranging from $7 to $12 USD for a hearty bowl. For an authentic experience, visitors should look for establishments known for their homemade dishes, as the best escabeche is prepared with care and served fresh. Enjoying this soup with a side of rice or fried plantains enhances the overall meal.

6.3 Seafood and Fresh Produce
Belize is a treasure trove of culinary delights, especially when it comes to seafood and fresh produce. Located between the Caribbean Sea and lush jungles, the country boasts an abundance of marine life and fertile land that together create a vibrant food scene. Visitors to Belize can expect to find an array of local seafood that is not only fresh but also rich in flavor, alongside an impressive variety of fruits and vegetables that reflect the region's agricultural diversity.

From bustling markets to charming roadside stalls, the opportunities to indulge in these local delicacies are plentiful.

Fresh Fish and Seafood Markets
In Belize, the heart of the seafood scene can be found in local fish markets, where vendors proudly display their daily catch. Popular spots include the fish market in Belize City and the San Pedro Fish Market on Ambergris Caye, where visitors can find an array of fresh fish, shrimp, conch, and lobster. Prices vary depending on the catch, with local snapper typically costing around $8 to $12 per pound, while lobsters may range from $10 to $15 per pound, depending on the season. Engaging with local fishermen can enhance the experience, as they often share stories about their daily catch and best cooking methods.

The Farmer's Market Experience
For those looking to immerse themselves in local culture, visiting farmer's markets is a must. The Belize City Farmer's Market, held on Saturdays, is a vibrant hub where vendors offer fresh fruits, vegetables, and homemade goods. Visitors can find an impressive selection of tropical fruits like mangoes, papayas, and pineapples, alongside organic vegetables such as tomatoes and cucumbers. Prices are generally affordable, with fresh produce often costing between $1 and $3 per item, making it an excellent option for budget-conscious travelers. Sampling local delicacies like tamales or fresh juices while exploring the market adds to the authentic experience.

Roadside Stalls and Restaurants
As you travel through Belize, roadside stalls and local eateries often present the freshest seafood and produce. These hidden gems serve up dishes made with ingredients sourced directly from nearby waters and fields. For instance, popular dishes such as ceviche, made from freshly caught fish and citrus, can be found for about $5 to $10 at local eateries. Engaging with the locals can lead to discovering the best spots for enjoying fresh seafood, and many vendors are happy to share recipes or preparation tips. Dining at these stalls not only supports the local economy but also offers an immersive cultural experience.

Gourmet Seafood Restaurants
For those seeking a more refined dining experience, Belize is home to several gourmet seafood restaurants that elevate local ingredients to new heights. Restaurants such as The Reef at the Radisson in Belize City feature menus

showcasing creative dishes like grilled lobster tails with garlic butter and pan-seared snapper with tropical salsa. Prices in these establishments can range from $15 to $40 per entree, reflecting the quality and presentation of the meals. Reservations are recommended, especially during peak tourist seasons, to ensure a memorable dining experience with stunning views of the Caribbean Sea.

Tips for Sourcing Fresh Ingredients
When sourcing seafood and fresh produce in Belize, it's essential to keep a few tips in mind. Always choose vendors that exhibit freshness in their offerings; fish should have a clean, ocean-like scent, while vegetables should be vibrant and firm. It's also advisable to ask about the catch of the day, as seasonal variations can affect availability and prices. Additionally, engaging with locals can provide insights into the best times to visit markets and stalls, as well as recommendations on how to prepare and enjoy these delightful ingredients. Embracing the local culinary scene will undoubtedly enhance your Belizean adventure.

6.4 Cooking Classes and Culinary Tours

Belize offers a unique opportunity for food enthusiasts to dive deep into its vibrant culinary heritage. With a rich tapestry of flavors influenced by its diverse cultures, cooking classes and culinary tours allow visitors to engage with local traditions while honing their culinary skills. These experiences not only provide practical cooking techniques but also a chance to connect with the heart of Belizean culture through its food. From traditional dishes to contemporary twists, exploring these cooking classes and tours will leave a lasting impression on any traveler.

Flavors of Belize Cooking School
Located in the charming town of San Ignacio, Flavors of Belize Cooking School is renowned for its immersive cooking experiences. The school offers hands-on classes where participants can learn to prepare traditional Belizean dishes such as rice and beans, stewed chicken, and fresh ceviche. Classes are typically priced around $75 per person, including all ingredients and a meal at the end. The school emphasizes the use of fresh, local produce, often sourced from nearby markets. For visitors, it's advisable to book in advance, especially during peak tourist seasons, to secure a spot in these popular classes. The friendly atmosphere and expert instruction ensure a delightful culinary journey.

Belize Culinary Adventures

Belize Culinary Adventures, based in Belize City, provides a unique blend of cooking classes and cultural immersion. Their tours often include visits to local markets where participants can select fresh ingredients before heading to the kitchen. Classes focus on classic Belizean recipes and range from $90 to $150 per person, depending on the specific tour and duration. Participants can expect not only to cook but also to learn about the cultural significance of each dish. A helpful tip for visitors is to wear comfortable clothing and shoes, as market visits can involve walking and exploration. This experience is perfect for those looking to understand the culinary landscape of Belize more intimately.

Taste Belize

Situated in the coastal paradise of Ambergris Caye, Taste Belize offers hands-on cooking classes that highlight the flavors of the Caribbean. Classes are typically priced around $80 per person and cover a variety of dishes, including seafood specialties that reflect the island's bounty. Visitors can expect a relaxed environment where they can learn about local ingredients and cooking methods. One of the key tips for participants is to engage with the instructors; they often share personal stories and traditions that enhance the overall experience. The combination of cooking with a scenic backdrop makes this an unforgettable culinary adventure.

The Maya Chef

The Maya Chef is a unique culinary experience located near the ancient ruins of Xunantunich. This cooking class focuses on traditional Maya cuisine, offering participants the chance to create authentic dishes such as tamales and cochinita pibil. Classes are reasonably priced at about $70 per person, and the experience often includes a guided tour of the nearby archaeological site. Visitors are encouraged to arrive early to enjoy the stunning views and historical context of the ruins. The emphasis on traditional cooking techniques not only teaches valuable skills but also connects participants to the rich history of the Maya civilization.

Cacao & Spice Cooking Class

For those with a sweet tooth, the Cacao & Spice Cooking Class in Punta Gorda is a delightful option. This unique class centers around Belize's rich cacao heritage, teaching participants how to create chocolate-based dishes alongside savory options. Priced at approximately $85 per person, this experience includes a visit to a local cacao farm, allowing participants to see the entire process from bean to bar. It's advisable to wear comfortable attire, as classes often involve hands-on activities that can get a bit messy. This class is perfect for anyone looking to indulge their senses while discovering the significance of cacao in Belizean culture.

6.5 Local Markets and Street Food

Belize is a vibrant country that boasts not only stunning natural landscapes but also a rich culinary heritage rooted in its diverse cultures. Exploring the local markets and street food scene provides an authentic taste of Belizean life, showcasing a variety of fresh produce, handmade goods, and delicious street snacks. These markets are not merely places to shop; they are lively hubs of culture, community, and tradition, where visitors can experience the true essence of Belize. From bustling city markets to quaint village stalls, each destination offers unique flavors and experiences that highlight the country's rich agricultural bounty.

Belize City's Collet Market
Located in the heart of Belize City, Collet Market is a bustling hub that reflects the vibrant daily life of locals. Open daily, this market is known for its colorful displays of fresh fruits, vegetables, and spices sourced from local farmers. Visitors can wander through the stalls, where they'll find an array of tropical fruits like juicy pineapples, mangos, and coconuts, alongside fresh herbs and vegetables. The market is also famous for its street food vendors, offering delights such as panades—savory fried pastries filled with fish or beans—and garnaches, which are fried tortillas topped with beans, cheese, and salsa. Engaging with the friendly vendors can provide insights into local culinary traditions and perhaps a few recipes to take home.

San Ignacio Market
The San Ignacio Market, situated in the charming town of San Ignacio, is another vibrant destination that draws locals and tourists alike. Open on Saturdays, this market is known for its lively atmosphere, filled with the sounds of vendors calling out their wares and the aromas of freshly cooked food. Here, visitors can explore an assortment of local produce, including organic vegetables and herbs, as well as artisanal products like handmade jewelry and crafts. A highlight of the market is the opportunity to sample local street foods, such as salbutes—crispy tortillas topped with meat and vegetables—and fresh juices

made from local fruits. The market is a perfect place to experience the warmth of Belizean hospitality while enjoying a true culinary adventure.

Punta Gorda's Fish Market
In the coastal town of Punta Gorda, the Fish Market offers a unique glimpse into the region's maritime culture. This market is renowned for its fresh seafood, as local fishermen bring in their daily catch, including snapper, lobster, and conch. The market operates early in the morning, making it a perfect spot for early risers looking to snag the freshest ingredients. Beyond seafood, visitors can also explore nearby stalls selling traditional Belizean street food, like fish tacos and ceviche, prepared right before their eyes. For those interested in cooking, chatting with the fishermen and vendors can provide valuable insights into the best methods for preparing the fresh catch, ensuring an authentic Belizean meal.

Cayo District Street Vendors
In the Cayo District, particularly in towns like Santa Elena and San Ignacio, street vendors serve up a delicious variety of local snacks that are a must-try for any visitor. These vendors often set up near parks or popular gathering spots, selling an array of treats such as empanadas, which are flaky pastries filled with meats or cheese, and coconut tartlets, a sweet dessert made with fresh coconut and spices. The prices are typically low, making it easy for visitors to sample a little bit of everything. Engaging with the vendors can also lead to interesting conversations about local customs and traditions, enriching the overall experience. This vibrant street food scene is perfect for those looking to enjoy a quick bite while exploring the picturesque landscapes of the Cayo District.

Belmopan Market
Belmopan, the capital city of Belize, features a local market that offers a delightful blend of fresh produce, meats, and local specialties. Known for its welcoming atmosphere, the Belmopan Market is a great place for visitors to discover the everyday life of Belizeans. The market is particularly vibrant on weekends when farmers and vendors from surrounding areas converge to sell their goods. Here, visitors can find everything from organic fruits and vegetables to homemade goods like salsas and pickles. The food stalls often serve traditional snacks such as tamales, which are masa dough filled with meats and wrapped in banana leaves, providing a flavorful and filling option for those on the go. Exploring this market allows visitors to not only taste local flavors but also understand the agricultural practices that sustain the Belizean community.

6.6 Nightlife and Entertainment

Belize is not only a paradise for nature lovers and history enthusiasts; it also offers a lively nightlife scene that captures the essence of Caribbean culture. As the sun sets, towns and cities come alive with music, dancing, and social gatherings. From beachfront bars to bustling nightclubs, Belize presents a diverse array of entertainment options that cater to various tastes and preferences. Exploring these nightlife spots provides visitors with an authentic taste of local culture, making for memorable evenings filled with fun and excitement.

The Rum Factory
Located just outside Belize City, The Rum Factory is a must-visit for those looking to immerse themselves in the local spirit culture. This establishment not only produces some of the finest rum in the region but also offers guided tours that explain the rum-making process. Visitors can enjoy tastings of different rums and learn about the history and significance of rum in Belizean culture. In the evenings, the factory transforms into a lively venue where guests can sample rum cocktails and enjoy live music, creating a festive atmosphere. With its rich flavors and warm ambiance, The Rum Factory is an excellent spot to unwind and connect with fellow travelers and locals alike.

Coco Beach Resort
Situated in the picturesque town of San Pedro on Ambergris Caye, Coco Beach Resort is known for its vibrant nightlife and beachfront parties. The resort frequently hosts themed nights and events, featuring live music, DJ performances, and dance parties that attract both guests and locals. The beachfront setting provides a stunning backdrop for evening festivities, allowing visitors to dance under the stars while enjoying tropical cocktails. With its laid-back yet lively vibe, Coco Beach Resort is the perfect place for those looking to socialize, relax, and enjoy the warm Caribbean breeze.

The Belize City Jazz Festival
Held annually in Belize City, the Belize City Jazz Festival is a highlight of the local entertainment scene, drawing music lovers from all over. The festival features a lineup of talented local and international jazz musicians who perform in various venues throughout the city. Visitors can enjoy a range of performances, from smooth jazz to energetic Latin rhythms, all while experiencing the vibrant atmosphere of the city. The festival typically takes

place during the summer months, and attending it allows visitors to immerse themselves in the rich musical heritage of Belize. Be sure to check the festival dates and plan accordingly to experience this unique celebration of jazz.

Putt Putt Golf & Bar
For a more unconventional nightlife experience, Putt Putt Golf & Bar in Belize City offers a fun and engaging way to spend an evening. This mini-golf venue features creatively designed courses that cater to players of all ages. As visitors navigate the whimsical obstacles, they can enjoy a selection of drinks and light bites from the bar, making for a relaxed yet entertaining atmosphere. Putt Putt often hosts themed nights and tournaments, encouraging friendly competition among guests. It's a great place for families or groups of friends looking for a unique evening out that combines laughter, skill, and good company.

The Blue Hole Dive Shop
While primarily known for its diving excursions, The Blue Hole Dive Shop in San Pedro also hosts lively events that cater to the nightlife crowd. After a day of exploring the underwater wonders of Belize, visitors can return to the shop for evening gatherings that often feature live music, trivia nights, and social mixers. This laid-back environment fosters connections among divers and travelers, providing an opportunity to share stories and experiences. The friendly staff and welcoming atmosphere make it a popular choice for those looking to unwind after a day of adventure, ensuring that every night is filled with laughter and camaraderie.

The Palace Theater
Located in Belize City, The Palace Theater is a historic venue that offers a glimpse into the cultural heart of the city. Known for its vintage charm, the theater hosts a variety of performances, including concerts, movie screenings, and cultural events. The theater's schedule is diverse, often featuring local talent and international acts that reflect the rich artistic landscape of Belize. For visitors, catching a show at The Palace Theater provides not only entertainment but also an opportunity to appreciate the local arts scene. With its cozy seating and intimate setting, the theater invites audiences to immerse themselves in the captivating performances that take center stage.

CHAPTER 7
DAY TRIPS AND EXCURSIONS

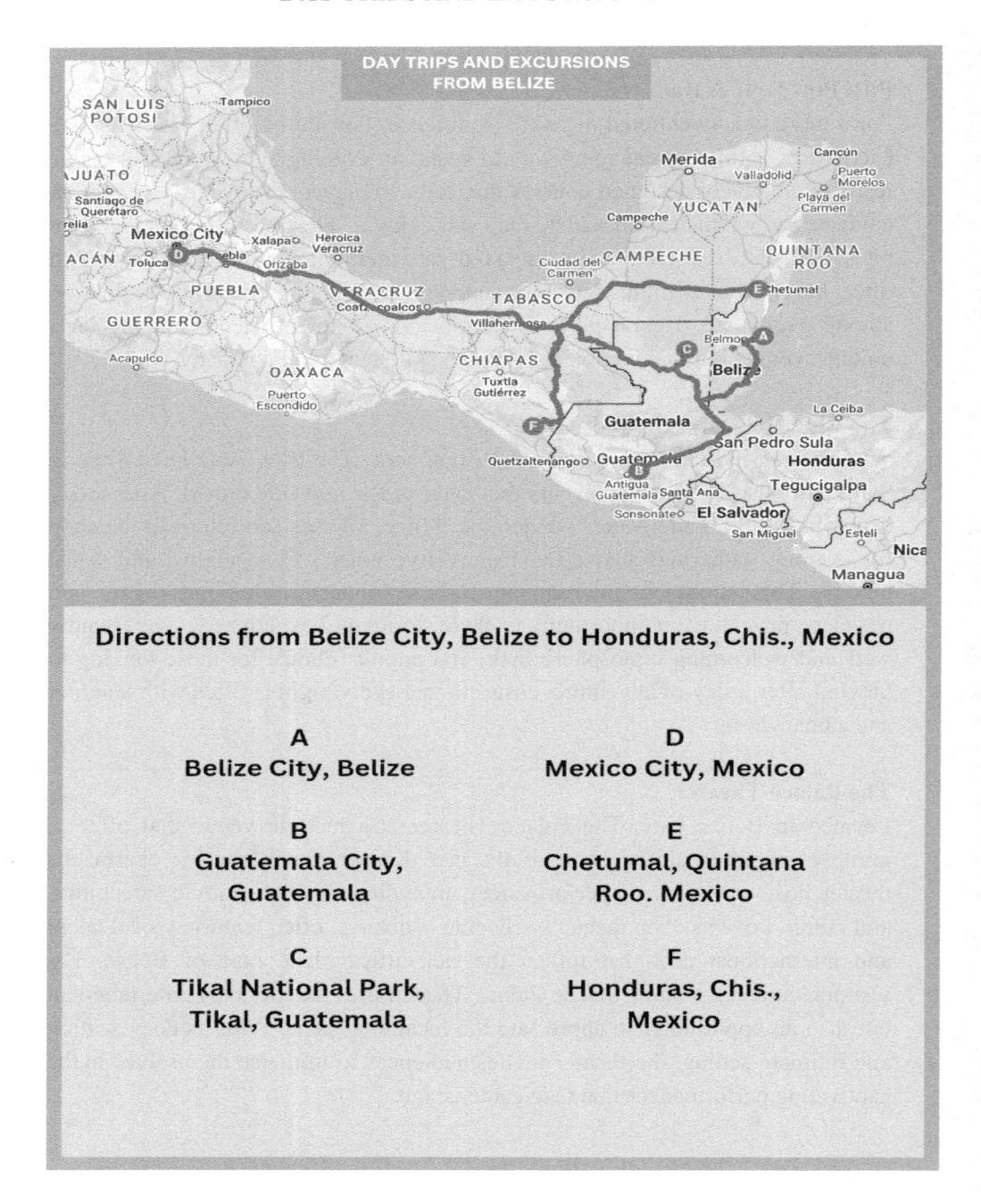

Directions from Belize City, Belize to Honduras, Chis., Mexico

A
Belize City, Belize

B
Guatemala City, Guatemala

C
Tikal National Park, Tikal, Guatemala

D
Mexico City, Mexico

E
Chetumal, Quintana Roo. Mexico

F
Honduras, Chis., Mexico

7.1 Guatemala Border and Tikal Ruins

Belize's proximity to Guatemala offers adventurous travelers a unique opportunity to explore the remarkable Tikal Ruins, one of the most significant archaeological sites of the ancient Maya civilization. Located within the lush jungles of Guatemala, Tikal is a UNESCO World Heritage site that boasts majestic pyramids, fascinating wildlife, and a rich tapestry of history. Excursions from Belize to Tikal provide a gateway to immerse yourself in the ancient world while experiencing the vibrant culture of the region.

Tikal

Located approximately 60 miles from the Belize-Guatemala border, Tikal is a sprawling site that features over 3,000 structures, including towering temples and sprawling plazas. As you approach the ruins, the sheer size and scale of the ancient city will take your breath away. The most iconic structures, such as Temple I and Temple II, rise dramatically above the jungle canopy, providing stunning vistas of the surrounding landscape. Visitors can explore the expansive grounds, where the sound of howler monkeys and the calls of exotic birds fill the air, creating a mesmerizing symphony of nature. Reaching Tikal from Belize typically involves a scenic drive through the countryside, often arranged as part of a guided tour. Tours usually depart from major towns like San Ignacio or Belize City and may include transportation, a knowledgeable guide, and admission fees. The journey typically takes around 1.5 to 2 hours, allowing you to soak in the beauty of the landscape as you pass through quaint villages and lush farmland. Be prepared for a border crossing, which may require a valid passport and a short wait.

The Journey to Tikal
The adventure to Tikal often begins with a journey to the Belize-Guatemala border. Depending on where you start, travelers can join organized tours that handle all the logistics, including border procedures. Most tours provide a comfortable van or bus ride, ensuring a hassle-free experience. The border crossing itself can be an interesting experience, as you'll witness the hustle and bustle of local life. It's essential to carry your passport and any required documents, and you might need to pay a small fee for the crossing. Once you cross into Guatemala, the scenery transforms, revealing more dramatic hills and dense jungles. The excitement builds as you approach Tikal, where your guide will provide insights into the history and significance of the ruins. The drive typically includes stops at local markets or points of interest, enhancing the overall experience. Some tours may also offer breakfast or lunch, allowing you to sample traditional Guatemalan cuisine, such as tamales or fresh fruit, before arriving at the site.

Exploring Tikal
Upon arrival at Tikal, visitors are greeted by the sight of ancient stone structures emerging from the jungle. A knowledgeable guide will lead you through the ruins, sharing fascinating stories about the Maya civilization, their architectural achievements, and their daily lives. Walking along the well-preserved paths, you'll encounter remarkable structures, including the massive Temple IV, which offers panoramic views of the surrounding rainforest. Ascending its steep steps is an experience in itself, as the breathtaking vistas reward your efforts. As you explore the various temples, plazas, and stelae, take a moment to appreciate the intricate carvings and hieroglyphs that adorn the stonework. Each tells a story of the Maya's complex society and their connection to the cosmos. Keep an eye out for the diverse wildlife that inhabits the area, including howler monkeys swinging through the trees and colorful toucans perched overhead. The natural beauty surrounding the ruins enhances the mystical atmosphere of Tikal, making it a truly unforgettable experience.

Practical Tips for Visiting Tikal
For those planning a day trip to Tikal from Belize, it's wise to prepare accordingly. Comfortable walking shoes are essential, as you'll be navigating

uneven terrain while exploring the site. Don't forget to bring plenty of water, sunscreen, and insect repellent, as the jungle can be hot and humid. A hat and lightweight clothing will also help keep you cool during your adventure. Most tours to Tikal offer a full day of exploration, allowing ample time to soak in the beauty of the ruins. However, some travelers may opt for a longer stay, as there are accommodations available near the site for those who wish to experience Tikal's magic during sunrise or sunset. Witnessing the sun rise over the ancient pyramids is a breathtaking sight that many find worth the extra time.

7.2 Mexico Border and Chetumal

Belize, with its rich cultural tapestry and stunning natural beauty, offers easy access to the neighboring country of Mexico, particularly the vibrant city of Chetumal. Day trips to the Mexican border and Chetumal provide visitors with an opportunity to immerse themselves in a different culture while enjoying a variety of experiences, from shopping and dining to exploring historical sites. These excursions are not only convenient but also deeply rewarding, allowing travelers to broaden their horizons without venturing too far from Belize.

Crossing into Mexico
The journey from Belize to Chetumal begins at the Belize-Mexico border crossing at Corozal, a mere 20 miles from the coastal town of Corozal. This small but bustling border town serves as a gateway for many travelers looking to

explore the Mexican side. The trip can be easily made by car, taxi, or local bus, with the drive taking about 30 to 45 minutes, depending on traffic and border wait times. Travelers should ensure they have their passports ready, as crossing into Mexico requires proper documentation. As you make your way to the border, the landscape transforms from the lush greenery of Belize to the more arid terrain of northern Quintana Roo, Mexico. The border crossing itself is relatively straightforward, and once you clear immigration, the excitement of stepping into another country sets in. You'll immediately notice the change in atmosphere, with signs in Spanish and a delightful mix of sounds and scents that beckon you to explore.

Discovering Chetumal
Chetumal, the capital of Quintana Roo, is a vibrant city that beautifully blends Mexican and Caribbean influences. Upon arriving, visitors are greeted by the picturesque views of the Chetumal Bay, with its tranquil waters and palm-fringed promenades. The city is known for its laid-back atmosphere, making it a perfect escape from the hustle and bustle of more tourist-heavy destinations. One of the must-visit spots in Chetumal is the Museum of Mayan Culture, where you can delve into the rich history of the ancient Maya civilization that once thrived in this region. The museum features intriguing exhibits, artifacts, and interactive displays that bring the past to life. After exploring the museum, a leisurely stroll along the waterfront promenade offers stunning views and a chance to enjoy local street food from various vendors. Try the tacos al pastor or fresh ceviche, which reflect the region's culinary diversity.

Shopping at Mercado Nuevo
A visit to Chetumal would not be complete without exploring Mercado Nuevo, a bustling market that showcases local crafts, fresh produce, and authentic Mexican goods. Here, visitors can browse through stalls filled with colorful textiles, handmade pottery, and intricate jewelry. The lively atmosphere is enhanced by the chatter of vendors and the aromas of freshly prepared food wafting through the air. Bargaining is a common practice here, so don't hesitate to engage with vendors to get the best deals. As you navigate through the market, take a moment to chat with locals, who are often eager to share their stories and recommendations. This interaction not only enriches your shopping experience but also fosters a deeper understanding of the local culture.

Scenic Spots and Relaxation

For those looking to unwind, Chetumal offers several beautiful parks and scenic spots. The Parque Integral de la Amistad is a favorite among both locals and visitors, featuring walking paths, playgrounds, and green spaces perfect for picnicking. The park is situated along the bay, providing a tranquil environment to relax and enjoy the view. If you're in the mood for a bit more adventure, consider taking a short boat ride to Bacalar Lagoon, known for its stunning blue waters and cenotes. This nearby destination is ideal for swimming, kayaking, and simply soaking in the natural beauty that surrounds you. The lagoon is a serene escape, allowing you to connect with nature while enjoying the tranquility of this hidden gem.

Returning to Belize

As your day in Chetumal comes to an end, retracing your steps back to the Belize border is just as easy. Remember to check the border hours and any potential wait times, especially during weekends and holidays when crossings can be busier. Once you cross back into Belize, you'll carry with you a wealth of experiences and memories from this delightful day trip.

7.3 Honduras Bay Islands

Belize's stunning coastal landscapes and vibrant marine ecosystems offer a gateway to the idyllic Honduras Bay Islands, a perfect destination for day trips and excursions. These islands provide a blend of adventure, relaxation, and cultural experiences, all while showcasing the breathtaking beauty of the Caribbean. Visitors to Belize will find that exploring these neighboring islands is a fantastic way to enhance their travel experience, with each excursion offering its unique charm and activities.

Roatan Island

Roatan Island, the largest of the Bay Islands, is renowned for its stunning beaches, lush landscapes, and world-class diving spots. Located approximately 40 miles from the coast of Belize, Roatan can be reached via a scenic ferry ride or a short flight from major Belizean cities like San Pedro or Belize City. The journey by ferry typically takes around an hour and offers breathtaking views of the Caribbean Sea. As you approach the island, you'll be captivated by the turquoise waters and vibrant coral reefs that surround this tropical paradise. Once on Roatan, visitors can indulge in a variety of activities, from snorkeling in the pristine waters of West Bay Beach to exploring the lush rainforests. The island is home to several dive shops offering guided tours to renowned dive sites, such as the famous Blue Hole and Half Moon Bay. For those interested in local culture, a visit to the Garifuna village of Punta Gorda provides insights into the island's rich heritage, complete with traditional music, dance, and cuisine. With its stunning natural beauty and warm hospitality, Roatan is a must-visit for anyone looking to escape to paradise.

Utila

Utila is the smallest of the Bay Islands and is known for its laid-back atmosphere, making it a popular destination for backpackers and adventure seekers. Located about 30 miles from the mainland of Honduras, Utila can be accessed via a short ferry ride or private boat from nearby Roatan. The journey typically takes around 45 minutes, allowing travelers to soak in the stunning scenery along the way.

Once you arrive on Utila, you'll find a world of opportunities for exploration and relaxation. The island is famous for its vibrant coral reefs, making it one of the top diving destinations in the world. Whether you're a seasoned diver or a beginner, Utila has dive shops that offer courses and guided dives, with the chance to see sea turtles, whale sharks, and colorful marine life. Beyond diving, visitors can enjoy snorkeling, kayaking, and hiking through the island's lush landscape. The local vibe is incredibly welcoming, and the nightlife is lively, with beachfront bars offering music, dancing, and a taste of local cuisine.

Cayos Cochinos
For those seeking an off-the-beaten-path experience, the Cayos Cochinos is a breathtaking archipelago located between Roatan and the mainland of Honduras. These unspoiled islands are a protected marine reserve, providing visitors with pristine beaches, vibrant coral reefs, and an abundance of wildlife. To reach Cayos Cochinos, travelers can book a day trip from Roatan, which typically includes a boat ride and guided exploration of the islands. Upon arrival, visitors can revel in the serene beauty of the Cayos Cochinos, where white-sand beaches meet crystal-clear waters. The islands offer excellent snorkeling opportunities, allowing you to swim among colorful fish and coral formations. Guided tours often include a stop at a local village, where you can learn about the unique culture and lifestyle of the indigenous Garifuna people. This excursion is perfect for those looking to disconnect from the hustle and bustle of daily life and immerse themselves in nature's tranquility.

Gumbalimba Park
Gumbalimba Park, located on Roatan Island, combines adventure and education in a stunning natural setting. Easily accessible from various points on the island, visitors can reach Gumbalimba Park via taxi or rental car. The park offers a wide range of activities, including zip-lining, animal encounters, and walking trails through lush gardens. As you explore the park, you'll encounter diverse wildlife, including monkeys, parrots, and iguanas. The zip-line tour is a highlight, providing an adrenaline-pumping experience as you soar above the treetops with breathtaking views of the Caribbean below. Gumbalimba Park also features a beautiful beach area, perfect for relaxing after a day of adventure. This destination is ideal for families and thrill-seekers alike, ensuring a day filled with fun and excitement.

Sandy Bay
Sandy Bay, located just a short drive from West End on Roatan, offers a quieter alternative to the more crowded beaches. This tranquil area is perfect for visitors seeking relaxation and natural beauty. Accessible by car or public transport, Sandy Bay is known for its calm waters, making it an excellent spot for swimming and snorkeling. Visitors can also explore the nearby Roatan Institute for Marine Sciences, which offers educational tours about marine conservation. The beach itself is lined with charming restaurants and bars, providing a perfect spot to enjoy a refreshing drink while taking in the serene surroundings.

CHAPTER 8
EVENTS AND FESTIVALS

8.1 Costa Maya Festival

Every August, the picturesque coastal town of San Pedro on Ambergris Caye transforms into a vibrant hub of culture, music, and tradition during the highly anticipated Costa Maya Festival. This annual event, which spans several days, serves as a celebration of the rich cultural heritage of Belize and the broader Central American region. As visitors flock to this idyllic island paradise, they are treated to a tapestry of experiences that highlight the traditions, flavors, and artistry of the region. Attending the Costa Maya Festival is not just about enjoying entertainment; it's an immersive journey into the heart of Belizean culture.

A Kaleidoscope of Culture

The Costa Maya Festival is unique in its dedication to showcasing the diverse cultures of Central America. Each year, the festival invites representatives from neighboring countries, including Mexico, Guatemala, and Honduras, to participate in a series of events and activities that reflect their unique traditions. This cultural exchange creates a vibrant atmosphere filled with colorful costumes, traditional dances, and local music that resonates throughout the streets of San Pedro. The festival typically kicks off with a spectacular parade that winds its way through the town, featuring beautifully decorated floats, traditional dancers, and musicians. Visitors are immediately drawn into the festive spirit, as the streets come alive with laughter, music, and the sounds of celebration. This initial spectacle sets the tone for the days to follow, encouraging attendees to explore the rich array of activities that await.

Gastronomic Delights
One of the festival's highlights is the opportunity to indulge in a diverse range of culinary offerings. Local vendors set up stalls throughout the festival grounds, serving an impressive selection of traditional Belizean dishes alongside regional delicacies from participating countries. From savory tamales and pupusas to fresh ceviche and grilled seafood, the festival is a paradise for food lovers. As the tantalizing aromas fill the air, visitors can engage with local chefs and learn about the preparation of traditional dishes, enhancing their appreciation for Belizean cuisine. Sampling these culinary delights not only satisfies the taste buds but also provides insight into the cultural significance of each dish. The blend of flavors and ingredients tells the story of a region rich in culinary heritage, making it an essential part of the festival experience.

Music and Dance
Music is the lifeblood of the Costa Maya Festival, with performances ranging from traditional folk music to contemporary genres. Local bands and artists take center stage, showcasing their talent and inviting the audience to join in the celebration. Whether it's the lively beats of Punta music or the soothing melodies of Garifuna songs, the performances are infused with the passion and rhythm that define Belizean culture. Visitors are often encouraged to participate in the festivities, whether by dancing along to the music or joining in traditional dance workshops. This interactive element fosters a sense of community and connection among attendees, allowing everyone to experience the joy of cultural expression firsthand. The festival's atmosphere is electric, with laughter, clapping, and cheers echoing throughout the night as the celebration continues under the stars.

Beauty Pageants and Cultural Showcase
One of the most anticipated events of the Costa Maya Festival is the Miss Costa Maya Pageant, where representatives from various countries compete for the crown. This pageant is not merely a beauty contest; it serves as a platform for

cultural representation and empowerment. Contestants showcase their cultural heritage through traditional attire and share their personal stories, highlighting the unique qualities of their respective nations. The pageant is a stunning visual experience, with vibrant costumes and elaborate designs that reflect the cultural richness of the region. As the contestants grace the stage, the audience is captivated by their poise and charisma. The event culminates in a celebration of unity and diversity, as the winner is crowned and honored for her commitment to cultural advocacy and community service.

Why Attend the Costa Maya Festival?
The Costa Maya Festival is not just an event; it is a celebration of life, culture, and community that offers visitors an opportunity to experience the heart and soul of Belize. The festival's enchanting blend of music, dance, culinary delights, and cultural exchange makes it a unique and memorable experience. Whether you are dancing to the rhythms of local bands, savoring traditional dishes, or connecting with locals and fellow travelers, the festival promises an unforgettable journey into the vibrant tapestry of Belizean life. As the festival draws near, travelers are encouraged to plan their visit to San Pedro and immerse themselves in this extraordinary celebration. The Costa Maya Festival stands as a testament to the resilience and vibrancy of Central American culture, inviting all who attend to join in the joyous festivities that define this magical time of year in Belize.

8.2 Belize City Carnival Road March

Every year, Belize City transforms into a vibrant tapestry of color, music, and unrestrained joy during the Belize City Carnival Road March. This exuberant event typically takes place in late September, coinciding with the country's Independence Day celebrations, and serves as a spirited lead-up to the main festivities. As the air fills with excitement and anticipation, locals and visitors alike prepare to join in a celebration that embodies the essence of Belizean culture and community.

A Vibrant Display of Culture
The Belize City Carnival is not just a parade; it is a dynamic showcase of Belizean heritage. The road march features an array of flamboyant costumes adorned with feathers, beads, and sequins, each more dazzling than the last. Participants, known as masqueraders, don these intricate outfits with pride, representing various groups and communities. The costumes often tell stories,

reflecting Belize's rich history, diversity, and cultural influences from the Garifuna, Mestizo, and Creole communities. As the day unfolds, the streets become a vibrant canvas filled with the laughter and excitement of revelers. The sound of infectious music—whether it's calypso, soca, or reggae—fills the air, encouraging everyone to dance and celebrate. Steel bands and live performances add to the electrifying atmosphere, inviting onlookers to join in the rhythmic movement of the carnival.

The Spirit of Unity and Celebration
What makes the Belize City Carnival Road March truly special is its spirit of unity. People from all walks of life come together to celebrate their shared culture and national pride. The sense of community is palpable, as friends, families, and visitors unite to partake in this joyous occasion. This gathering transcends differences, creating an inclusive environment where everyone is welcome to join in the festivities. The energy is infectious; as the procession moves through the streets, laughter and cheers echo from all corners. Food vendors line the route, offering a variety of delicious Belizean dishes—from spicy tamales to sweet coconut treats—ensuring that the flavors of Belize accompany the visual feast. This celebration of culture is not just about visual spectacle; it's also a sensory delight that captures the essence of Belizean life.

A Day to Remember
Attending the Belize City Carnival Road March is an experience unlike any other. As a visitor, you are invited to immerse yourself in the festivities, feeling the rhythm of the drums reverberate through your body and the excitement of the crowd sweep you off your feet. The atmosphere is charged with a sense of freedom and celebration that encourages even the most reserved individuals to join in the dance. The parade's route winds through the heart of the city, allowing spectators to witness the transformation of everyday streets into a vibrant carnival landscape. As the march progresses, you'll see families adorned in matching outfits, children waving flags, and adults donning masks, all celebrating together in a colorful display of joy and unity.

Worth Every Moment
The Belize City Carnival Road March is more than just a festival; it is a living testament to the resilience and vibrancy of Belizean culture. It offers a unique opportunity for visitors to engage with locals, learn about the traditions that shape the nation, and create lasting memories. Whether you are participating in

the parade, dancing along the sidelines, or simply soaking in the festive atmosphere, each moment spent at the carnival is worth every bit of time.

8.3 Garifuna Settlement Day

Garifuna Settlement Day, celebrated on November 19th each year, is a vibrant and deeply significant festival that honors the arrival of the Garifuna people in Belize. This annual event not only marks a pivotal moment in the country's history but also serves as a colorful celebration of Garifuna culture, music, dance, and culinary traditions. Held in various locations, with the largest festivities taking place in Dangriga, the festival attracts both locals and visitors eager to experience the rich heritage of the Garifuna community.

A Rich Historical Context

The significance of Garifuna Settlement Day lies in its historical roots. The Garifuna people, descendants of West African, Arawak, and Carib ancestors, were exiled from their homeland on the island of St. Vincent in 1797 and eventually made their way to Central America, including Belize. The festival commemorates their journey, resilience, and the establishment of their communities along the Caribbean coast. It serves as a reminder of their enduring spirit and cultural legacy, creating a sense of pride among Garifuna descendants and fostering appreciation among others.

A Festive Atmosphere

As the day approaches, the atmosphere in Dangriga and other Garifuna communities becomes electric with anticipation. On the morning of November 19th, colorful parades fill the streets, featuring traditional costumes, lively drumming, and energetic dancing. The sound of punta music—a genre that is both rhythmic and celebratory—fills the air, inviting everyone to join in the festivities. Attendees can witness traditional dance performances, where dancers gracefully move to the beats of drums, showcasing the unique Garifuna rhythm and storytelling through movement. The festival is a visual feast, with vibrant banners, decorations, and the colors of the Garifuna flag prominently displayed. The joyous spirit of the celebration resonates through the laughter and camaraderie shared among attendees, creating an inclusive environment that welcomes all.

Culinary Delights and Cultural Exhibitions
No celebration would be complete without food, and Garifuna Settlement Day offers a delectable array of traditional dishes. Visitors can indulge in mouthwatering meals such as hudut (a fish stew served with mashed plantains), cassava bread, and various seafood delicacies. Food stalls line the streets, offering a tantalizing selection of local flavors that highlight the unique culinary traditions of the Garifuna community. Sampling these dishes not only satisfies the palate but also deepens the understanding of Garifuna heritage.

Cultural exhibitions play a crucial role in the festival, with displays of traditional crafts, art, and storytelling. Local artisans showcase their talents through handmade jewelry, clothing, and artwork, providing insight into the rich cultural expressions of the Garifuna people. Workshops and demonstrations further engage attendees, allowing them to learn about Garifuna music, dance, and traditional practices firsthand.

Why It's Worth Attending
Attending Garifuna Settlement Day is an experience unlike any other. It offers visitors a chance to immerse themselves in the vibrant culture of the Garifuna people, fostering a deeper appreciation for their history and traditions. The festival is not merely a celebration; it is a testament to the resilience and strength of a community that has preserved its identity through generations. Moreover, the warmth and hospitality of Garifuna people create an inviting atmosphere for everyone. Visitors are encouraged to participate in the dances, share in the meals, and engage in conversations with community members. This sense of connection and belonging transcends cultural boundaries, making the festival a truly enriching experience. As the sun sets, the festivities continue with live music, dance performances, and community gatherings that resonate with the joyous spirit of the day. The vibrant energy of Garifuna Settlement Day lingers in the hearts of all who attend, leaving lasting memories and a profound respect for the Garifuna culture.

8.4 Lobster Fest
Lobster Fest in Belize is a vibrant and mouthwatering celebration that highlights the country's rich culinary traditions and the bountiful treasures of its coastal waters. This annual event takes place during the summer months, specifically in June and July, aligning with the beginning of the lobster season. As the local fishermen set out to catch the freshest lobsters, communities along the coast

prepare for a feast that attracts both locals and tourists alike. The festival is not just about the delicious seafood; it is a celebration of Belizean culture, community, and the joy of sharing good food.

The Essence of Lobster Fest
At its core, Lobster Fest is a gastronomic delight, showcasing an array of dishes that elevate the humble lobster to culinary heights. From grilled lobsters seasoned with traditional spices to lobster ceviche and lobster tacos, the festival presents a diverse menu that caters to all tastes. Local chefs often experiment with flavors, incorporating Belizean ingredients such as cilantro, lime, and coconut to create unique dishes that tantalize the palate. As you wander through the festival, the tantalizing aroma of grilled seafood fills the air, enticing attendees to indulge in a culinary adventure. Beyond the food, what makes Lobster Fest truly special is the sense of community it fosters. Towns such as San Pedro on Ambergris Caye and Caye Caulker transform into lively hubs of activity during the festival. Streets come alive with music, dancing, and laughter as locals and visitors gather to celebrate together. The festival often features live bands playing a mix of traditional and contemporary music, creating an energetic atmosphere that invites everyone to join in the festivities. This vibrant spirit of camaraderie is palpable, making Lobster Fest a memorable experience for all who attend.

A Unique Cultural Experience
Attending Lobster Fest is not just about enjoying great food; it is also an opportunity to immerse oneself in the rich culture of Belize. The festival often includes cultural performances, showcasing traditional dance and music that reflect the country's diverse heritage. Local artisans display their crafts, offering visitors a chance to take home a piece of Belizean culture. From handwoven textiles to intricate jewelry, the festival serves as a platform for local artists to shine and share their creations with a broader audience. The event also emphasizes sustainability and responsible fishing practices. Many local organizations participate in discussions and workshops during the festival, educating attendees about the importance of protecting marine life and preserving the environment.

Why It's Worth Attending
For anyone visiting Belize during the summer months, Lobster Fest is an unmissable experience. The festival offers a chance to savor some of the freshest

and most delicious seafood in the Caribbean, all while enjoying the lively atmosphere that characterizes Belizean culture. The sense of community, combined with the opportunity to engage with local traditions and culinary delights, creates an experience that goes beyond a typical food festival. Moreover, the picturesque backdrop of Belize's stunning coast enhances the charm of Lobster Fest. Whether you find yourself on the sandy beaches of Caye Caulker or the bustling streets of San Pedro, the natural beauty of the surroundings complements the celebration. Imagine sipping a refreshing rum punch while watching the sunset over the Caribbean, the sound of laughter and music in the air, and the tantalizing taste of fresh lobster lingering on your palate.

8.5 Christmas in Belize

Christmas in Belize is a magical time that blends rich cultural traditions with the warmth of community spirit. This festive season typically begins in early December and culminates in vibrant celebrations on Christmas Eve and Christmas Day. As the country prepares for the holiday, the atmosphere transforms into one filled with joy, music, and a sense of togetherness that captivates both locals and visitors alike. Experiencing Christmas in Belize offers a unique perspective on the holiday, making it a worthwhile endeavor for anyone seeking to immerse themselves in a different cultural celebration.

The Spirit of the Season

As December approaches, towns and villages throughout Belize come alive with decorations that reflect the holiday spirit. Colorful lights adorn homes and public spaces, while festive wreaths and nativity scenes add a touch of tradition. The air is filled with the tantalizing aromas of traditional foods being prepared, such as tamales, fruitcake, and the beloved black cake, which is rich with fruits soaked in rum. These culinary delights are often enjoyed during family gatherings, where loved ones come together to share stories and laughter, reinforcing the importance of community ties. In many Belizean communities, the holiday season is marked by the joyful sounds of music and dance. Local musicians play traditional tunes, often featuring the lively rhythms of punta and soca, inviting everyone to join in the festivities. The celebration is not just confined to Christmas Eve; it extends throughout the month, with numerous events, parades, and parties that bring people together. This vibrant energy creates a welcoming atmosphere that is infectious, making it a perfect time for visitors to join in and experience the local culture firsthand.

Christmas Eve
Christmas Eve, known as "Nochebuena," is particularly special in Belize, as families prepare for a night of celebration that lasts until the early hours of Christmas Day. In many households, the evening begins with a festive meal, where families gather around tables laden with traditional dishes. Tamales, often filled with chicken or pork, are a favorite, along with rice and beans, and seasonal fruits. As they feast, families share stories, sing carols, and exchange gifts, creating lasting memories that will be cherished for years to come. The night is also marked by the sound of firecrackers, which are lit to ward off evil spirits and celebrate the joyous occasion. This lively display of lights and sounds can be witnessed throughout the streets, adding to the festive ambiance. In some towns, midnight Mass is a cherished tradition, where the community comes together to celebrate the birth of Christ, creating a sense of unity and reverence amid the festive revelry. Attending a Christmas Eve service in Belize can be a profound experience, offering a glimpse into the spiritual aspect of the holiday.

Christmas Day
Christmas Day in Belize is a continuation of the festivities, filled with laughter, music, and more delicious food. Families often begin the day by attending church services, followed by a celebratory brunch or lunch that features a variety of traditional dishes. The mood is one of joy and gratitude, with families coming together to share their blessings and enjoy the company of loved ones. Children play in the streets, often showing off new toys received from Santa, while adults engage in friendly conversations and laughter. The sense of community is palpable, as neighbors visit one another, exchanging good wishes and treats. The day is often spent in leisure, with many families heading to the beach or local parks to enjoy the beautiful tropical weather. This laid-back atmosphere provides a refreshing contrast to the hustle and bustle often associated with the holiday season elsewhere.

Why It's Worth Attending
Experiencing Christmas in Belize offers visitors a unique opportunity to witness the country's diverse cultural tapestry woven into the fabric of the holiday. The celebrations are a reflection of the nation's rich history, encompassing influences from the Garifuna, Mestizo, and Creole communities, each contributing their own customs and traditions. This multicultural experience not only enhances the festive atmosphere but also provides an enriching experience for those who

partake. Visitors will find that the warmth and hospitality of the Belizean people make it an unforgettable time to explore the country. Engaging with locals during this season allows travelers to participate in various community events, from parades to cultural showcases, fostering connections that go beyond typical tourist experiences. Whether you're enjoying a festive meal, dancing to local music, or simply soaking in the vibrant atmosphere, Christmas in Belize is a celebration that resonates with joy, warmth, and a true sense of belonging.

INSIDER TIPS AND RECOMMENDATIONS

When it comes to tropical paradises, Belize stands out as a hidden gem, beckoning travelers with its stunning landscapes, vibrant culture, and unparalleled biodiversity. As you close the pages of "Belize Travel Guide 2025 and Beyond," a world of vibrant cultures, breathtaking landscapes, and unforgettable adventures awaits you. This guide has illuminated the hidden gems and iconic treasures of Belize, offering insights that will inspire and prepare you for the journey of a lifetime. Each destination within this enchanting country is more than just a place on the map; it is a canvas of experiences that tells a story, invites connection, and beckons you to explore its wonders. From the lush rainforests to the azure waters of the Caribbean, Belize promises a rich tapestry of moments that will linger in your heart long after you've returned home. Belize is a land of contrasts, where ancient Mayan ruins rise majestically from the earth, whispering tales of a bygone civilization, while vibrant markets pulse with life, showcasing the warmth and spirit of its people. The moment you set foot in this tropical paradise, you'll feel an invigorating energy that draws you into its embrace. The blend of cultures here—Mayan, Garifuna, Creole, and Mestizo—creates a vibrant atmosphere that is both welcoming and enriching. You will savor the mouthwatering cuisine, immerse yourself in the rhythms of local music, and form friendships that will make you feel at home, no matter where you come from. As you embark on your journey through this Central American haven, remember to approach each experience with an open heart and a curious mind. Explore the wonders of the Great Blue Hole, an underwater marvel that invites both novice and experienced divers to discover its breathtaking beauty. Traverse the winding trails of the lush jungles, where the calls of exotic birds and the rustle of wildlife create a symphony that only nature can orchestrate. Whether you're lounging on the sun-kissed beaches of Ambergris Caye or hiking through the serene landscapes of the Mountain Pine Ridge Forest Reserve, every moment spent in Belize is an opportunity to connect with the extraordinary.

For those planning their adventure, consider this a heartfelt recommendation: make your travel plans sooner rather than later. Belize's charm lies not just in its picturesque views but in the genuine hospitality of its people and the experiences that await you. Timing your visit to coincide with local festivals can add an extra layer of excitement, as you'll have the chance to celebrate alongside the community, tasting traditional dishes and participating in time-honored rituals. The Belize Carnival and the September Celebrations offer a vibrant glimpse into the culture that defines this beautiful country. When it comes to accommodations, let your preferences guide you. Whether you seek luxury in a beachfront resort or the cozy charm of a guesthouse, Belize offers a spectrum of options tailored to your taste and budget. Planning your itinerary with a balance of adventure, relaxation, and cultural immersion will ensure you leave with a well-rounded understanding of this incredible destination. In your travels, embrace the unexpected. Sometimes, the most memorable experiences arise from spontaneous moments—striking up a conversation with a local vendor, getting lost in a bustling market, or simply watching the sunset paint the sky in hues of orange and pink. Each day in Belize is a new opportunity to create lasting memories, and by stepping outside your comfort zone, you'll discover facets of the country that guidebooks often overlook. As you reflect on the contents of this travel guide, let it serve as a reminder that adventure is calling. Belize is not just a destination; it is a journey of discovery that will leave an indelible mark on your soul.

So pack your bags, gather your loved ones, and set forth to experience the magic of Belize. With its lush landscapes, rich culture, and boundless adventures, you'll find that Belize is a treasure waiting to be uncovered. Your story in Belize is waiting to be written—don't let it be just a chapter in a book; let it be the adventure of a lifetime. The beauty of Belize awaits; it's time to make it yours.

Made in United States
Orlando, FL
12 April 2025